How to
TAME LIONS

---

and other great yarns

MAX WALKER

Publications

Garry Sparke and Associates
P.O. Box 360, Glen Waverley, Victoria 3150

First published 1988
© Max Walker.

Typesetting by GS Typesetting
Printed by Magenta Press.
40 Geddes St., Mulgrave.

ISBN 0 908081 75 8

Foreword
by Lou Richards

Back in the late sixties when Melbourne footy club was the chopping block side of the VFL, they scoured Australia for big men.

From Tasmania they recruited a sapling named Max Walker . . . a tall, gangling kid with a style of his own . . . and they thrust him onto the unsuspecting Melbourne audiences in 1967.

When I first saw him wearing that number one jumper, I thought he was a big log. After all, I've never had any time for ruckmen.

I've lived by the adage, "A good little man will run rings around a good big man" and the Demons' would be super-star ruckman added weight to the theory. Max never really made it as a ruckman, although the record shows 93 games, but as a Test cricketer he was a breath of fresh air . . .

He developed a magic rapport with the crowds, with his team-mates and the opposition and with that huge Tasmanian smile and the long Tasmanian drawl, added warmth and humour to the game.

He bobbed up at Channel 7, Melbourne, one Sunday morning to appear as the cricket expert on the long-running, but now defunct World of Sport.

Crikey, he was as bad on television as he was on the football field, but everyone liked his relaxed, laid back style.

The boys played every joke on him; they shuffled his cue cards, set fire to his idiot sheets and bared their bums as he went live to air. It was a tough initiation and 'Tangles' came through with flying colours.

We teamed up again under a new banner, on Wide World of Sports in 1987, and have enjoyed hosting the Sunday morning edition of the best national sports show in the land.

For a big bloke he's not all that bad. He loves a yarn and doesn't mind tempering the truth a little . . . how about the title of the book? Fair dinkum, I was in the cage with him and there is no way either of us had anything on our minds except escape! But why ruin a good story with facts, after all, it hasn't worried me for 30 years . . .

LOU RICHARDS
Toorak, 1988

Introduction

Before I introduce 'How to Tame Lions', I want to say thank you very much to the tens of thousands of people who enjoyed reading 'How to Hypnotise Chooks' and in doing so, have provided the catalyst to make this new book happen.

It would appear that there are many people who share my warped sense of humour and an immense enjoyment of life and its situations. So again, this new book is basically an anecdotal romp.

I genuinely love meeting and talking to people and I'm lucky enough to be able to continue to meet a large cross section of the community — sharing their thoughts and experiences — as part of my occupation in the media.

Today my commitments focus on television as co-host of Channel 9's 'Wide World of Sports'. However, I still get a great satisfaction working in radio, making word pictures — in television the pictures are already there. To be able to travel the length and breadth of our beautiful sunburnt continent to speaking engagements is a constant source of excitement and subject matter to write about . . . as in this book.

I love writing but somehow there just doesn't seem to be enough hours in the day. I find there are many differences in writing for television and radio. Putting ideas and stories on paper for a book and writing just for fun also varies.

My objective is to write like I speak and speak like I write and it's not easy to achieve. Still, I keep on seeking to get better, looking for new ways to improve my skills of communication.

My dad, known as 'Big Max' still 'hates' an audience and enjoys nothing better than stretching the truth to get a laugh. From my early formative years he continually encouraged me to laugh . . . to look for the lighter, richer side of life; it truly has been a great philosophy. Somehow the problems and burdens don't seem quite as worrying if you can laugh or smile at yourself.

I've done exactly that in this collection of stories.

Many of the laughs come also from close friends and acquaintances; cab drivers and parking inspectors; cricketers and footballers. A laugh can happen anywhere . . . get one inside the cover of this book.

Max

CONTENTS

Chapter One

ALL IN A DAY'S WORK

Everyone fell about laughing as I strained to concentrate on my line.

Giving 'em Plenty of Lip
'HE BARELY KNEW WHICH END OF A CRICKET BAT TO PICK UP'

On March the 15th, 1923, when the doctor delivered Louis Thomas Charles Richards, they tell me it only took one smack on his bare bottom and a quick flip upside down to get that cute little mouth to make a noise!

And ever since that day, Louie has been making a lot of noise. Hundreds of thousands of people from Cape York, Queensland to Broome in the West have become fans of this lovable little fella from the back streets of Collingwood where corrugated iron rooftops are painted black and white. Yes Lou Richards epitomised the miner's cottage and chimney stack tradition that made the Collingwood Football Club famous.

These days Louie is a very successful television personality and businessman. He's immaculately dressed, thanks to his lovely wife Edna (Lou wouldn't admit it but the whisper is . . . she even selects his underpants! C'mon Lou who does wear the pants in your house?) and sports a very distinguished shock of silver hair. But it wasn't always easy! In those rough and ready days of the 40's and 50's there were no fashion garments and tailored clothing, only a set of overalls and a gladstone bag.

Australian rules football was his game and boy, could the little bloke play. He kicked off his career in 1941, just a couple of drop kicks away from home. He loved to win and win they did. In an incident-packed career that finished in 1955, Louie had chalked up 250 VFL games with Collingwood. Only three other men have represented his beloved club more often at Victoria Park.

It was fitting that this home grown product — educated at Collingwood Tech where his algebra might not have been up to standard, but learnt a lot about bloodied knee caps, dirty faces and how to get a football when the going gets tough — should climb to the role of captain in 1952 and lead the side to a premiership over Geelong the following year.

There's no doubt about Lou, you either love him or hate him. He'd be the first to admit he's upset plenty over the journey which took him into the heart and soul of Melbourne's football media machine — as an outlandish journalist with the Melbourne Sun and focus for HSV 7's one and only 'World of Sport'. It's not surprising then that he didn't win Collingwood's Copeland Trophy for the FAIREST as well as the best player!

Louie's quick wit and acid tongue has got him into and out of plenty of hot water. Maybe that's where one of his many nicknames — Louie The Lip — originated.

A man of his word and conviction, there's never a dull moment . . . he believes strongly in a football team's ability to win and is hardly ever right.

7

He once told me he picked all six winners in a VFL round more than 20 years ago! That's a bit rough when the legend is supposed to be a football expert!

League coaches hate him to select their team to win because he's so often wrong — the 'Kiss of Death' it's called. Sometimes he is committed enough to categorically state something stupid like jumping off the end of Brighton pier at 6.00 a.m. on a freezing mid-July morning — if he is wrong.

As he dragged himself from the icy waters of Port Phillip Bay a couple of decades back, without a wet suit, he muttered: "I'll never do that again . . . can't be good for a bloke's sex life being this counter sunk!"

Several months later 'Louie the Lip' had cracked it for another big one . . . this time sweeping Bourke Street, Melbourne, with a plastic toothbrush. It took a while!

He is one of the great characters of Melbourne and has been named King of Moomba like Graham Kennedy, Mickey Mouse, tennis player Paul McNamee and that bulbous actor with the very proper voice, Frank Thring.

In the early 80's I was invited to become Channel 7's cricket expert on World of Sport. I was a little apprehensive at first because the show had been running for 20 odd years with most of the same people in the same format. Good luck Maxie, I thought. I was to need some too!

At Dorcas Street, South Melbourne — in a large barn like warehouse — I was to experience first hand the on camera and behind the scenes pranks of Lou Richards and his co-stars.

The first week of appearing on tele was a pretty hair-raising experience. No instruction, no coaching, pick your own subject, talk when the red light starts flashing on the camera.

Everyone else on the floor in the spartan old studios was joking, laughing and generally uninterested in what I was about to say. After all, 'district cricket' wasn't exactly the sort of television viewing that would make you put off going to make a cup of coffee or drop the washing up to turn around to see who had won in the match between Footscray and South Melbourne.

Actually during my inaugural 'piece' to camera, I took a long, large nervous breath . . . and before I could make a second, hard-hitting point, the director, like God almighty somewhere upstairs in the control room, had slipped in a commercial break.

Now I should explain there is a lot of difference between being asked questions in an interview situation and being the up front person making the sensible comments as well as asking the pertinent questions, particularly if the first two or three thought-provoking prodders manage only a blunt "Yes", or "No" as a response! So to perform articulately, and at the same time making sense for say, three minutes, is a very difficult assignment.

GTV 9 newsreader Brian Naylor speaks at approximately five words per second. Yours truly is a fair degree slower at three per second — most Tasmanians do speak slowly. As you can imagine, sitting in front of camera as a terrified and nervous new presenter, 180 seconds can seem like an energy sapping 500 metre dash. It never ends!

Sometimes things don't quite go as planned . . . and that's when life really gets interesting. For example, the totally unexpected happened during my second weekend at Dorcas Street, much to everyone else's delight.

The culprit was one of Louie's best mates, a grotesque, bespectacled man, tipping the scales at more than 20 stone and affectionately referred to as 'Uncle Doug' or 'Unca!' He was one of the foundation members of this historic television program and over the 28 years of the show's lifetime, Doug Elliott was the bloke most likely to plug the products. He would be Mr Patra orange juice, Mr Red Tulip Chocolates . . . cheese, meat . . . you name it, Unc would be flogging as hard as his firm jaw and shaking his head would allow.

A former Lord Mayor of Essendon, he had a sharp wit and penchant for poetry which he often read on air. The big fella's appetite was legendary . . it was stated often that if they X-rayed Unc's stomach they'd find three or four meat pies nestled comfortably inside without even a tooth mark on 'em! He wasn't a guts as some of his mates often suggested . . . merely a not so fussy connoisseur of all edible sponsor products.

Like most of 'the team' Unc loved a practical joke. I do as long as I'm not the subject. Unfortunately as the new boy on the show my 'initiation' on the set was going to be much fun for everyone but Channel Seven's brand new cricket expert.

After less than 30 seconds regurgitating several well rehearsed comments on the leadership qualities of the blue-eyed boy from the West — Kimberley Hughes — a pear-shaped man with thick rimmed glasses appeared camera right. I couldn't believe my eyes!

Now I don't wish to sound rude and crude but this was how it was. Uncle Doug brazenly stood in my line of sight and slowly, animatedly undid the belt holding up his badly creased trousers. At this stage I was in a state of confusion . . . should I ignore him and continue trying to make sense to the totally unaware audience? I tried for a few more uncomfortable seconds.

Then it all became too much when his trousers slipped past his nobbly kneecaps into a crumpled pile around his ankles, followed by his Hawthorn underpants — you know the type — yellow in the front and brown stains on the back.

I had a grin like Luna Park and the laughter was hard to suppress. Remember, there was no seven seconds delay, this was pure, live television. Without even thinking, I'd blurted: "I don't believe it . . . he's just dropped his dacks!"

His reaction was to about face and touch his toes. They were the worst set of hamstrings I had seen in many, many years — completely devoid of muscle tone and polar bear white in colour.

Meanwhile cameras were jockeying for position like dodgem cars with a view to capturing the mature gentleman dragging his trousers up to somewhere above the 'plimsol line'. I've never seen a pair of trousers and fly zip hoisted so quickly on the silver screen.

Yes, it was a memorable second day at HSV 7.

After my 'initiation' Uncle Doug wrapped his arm around my shoulder: "That was great son, spontaneity is what this caper is all about . . . the show thrives on it!"

How true these words were. World of Sport was the only live television show I know that could be running 30 minutes behind schedule after only being on air for an hour — the madcap ad lib and semi-organised 'chaos' was half the charm and attraction of this almost compulsory Victorian Sunday viewing.

Day number three at the station turned out to be just as exciting — my motto should have been "prepare for the unexpected".

This time Lou got into the act . . . again yours truly was on the receiving end.

Many people had suggested Louie the Lip wouldn't be super helpful . . . after all, he barely knew which end of a cricket bat to pick up but he had done a lot of miles in front of camera. So when the chunky little ex-rover from Magpieland offered some advice, I thought, don't be quick to judge, maybe he's genuine. The straight look on his face was too serious to believe — but gullible old me did. This rough-hewn, loudly spoken master of the ad-lib suggested I use an 'idiot sheet' like all the pros — Don Lane, Bert Newton and Mike Walsh.

My basic problem was not being able to say "Goodbye" quickly. In other words, they couldn't shut me up! Lou thought that if I was scripted, the problem wouldn't arise. How the shoe is on the other foot these days at GTV 9. My little mate is still having trouble distinguishing the difference between a 13 second chat and a 49 second conversation. We see that familiar 'wind-up' hand movement from the floor manager just about every story. We both like to have a chat!

At the completion of my District Cricket segment, Louie stood next to the camera, legs slightly astride, arms high with a huge sheet of butcher's paper. In the corner of his mouth his cigarette began to glow a bright red as he inhaled quickly. His mischievous eyes were dancing left and right looking for attention . . . he had all the support he needed.

My old architecture lecturer, Ron Centre, would have been proud of the lovely lettering on the beige coloured paper. This graduate from Collingwood Tech had obviously set down with a chunky felt pen and neatly written my closing message.

What a lovely gesture, I thought, as I began to read, word perfect "Well, that just about wraps up the District Cricket . . . "

I never did make it to the end of line two because quick as a flash, Lou had dug deep into his Christian Dior trouser pocket and produced a cigarette lighter — no ordinary lighter either — a Dunhill, thank you very much! A sure sign the boy from the back streets of Collingwood had a few bob to spend on himself. Well, he doesn't spend it on anyone else!

What do you reckon he did with the tiny gold flame-thrower? You guessed it! He licked the bottom corners of the paper sign with the flame . . . everyone fell about laughing as I strained to concentrate on my line. Within seconds, the bottom half of the script was going up in smoke and Louie began to cough loudly.

" . . . someone call the fire brigade . . . and avagoodweegend!!" was about the best I could think of as a quick out.

Well a lot of water flowed down the gutters of Melbourne in the next six years — both Lou and myself crossed the tramlines to join the sports team at Channel 9 and still the fun continues.

After watching a troup of female body builders complete their routines for the world title one morning on Wide World of Sports 'Sunday Edition', I asked Lou a simple straightforward question: "What did you think of Dianne — the one in the orange bikini?"

After one more squinted look at our TV monitor, Lou let loose with a rip snorter of a reply: "She'd be pretty handy on a half-back flank for Collingwood wouldn't she?"

Needless to say we had about a hundred letters about his tactless quip . . . but at the time Collingwood weren't winning too many games and he probably meant it.

Just like the full mug of coffee the little bugger poured over me during a commercial break . . . everywhere, shirt, tie, jacket, trousers. He was still apologising for making my underpants hot and sticky and I found it very hard to keep a straight face as the floor manager counted me in: 5, 4, 3, 2, 1 and his arm dropped! The light was on and away I went introducing the next story.

Then he dared me to introduce the following part of the show — trouserless! In other words blazer and tie . . . and underpants! "Go on," he said. "You're gutless."

It never ends. The chatter is constant. "Did ya hear the one about the two hard-boiled eggs on their wedding night . . . ?"

I'd heard that one 45 times, but with a new cameraman on duty he's worth a try, well, that's Lou's theory!

Louie had once asked a question of a presenter knowing the segment was taped. Then had the audacity to reckon the bloke had the 'tom tits' with him . . . and wouldn't answer.

No doubt about it, there's never a dull or quiet moment with my little mate, 'Louie the Lip'.

How to Tame Lions

'IT'S NOT THAT MY LITTLE MATE HAD A WEAK BLADDER, HE WAS GENUINELY TERRIFIED . . .'

Commonsense should have prevented us entering the lions' cage but it didn't — I guess that is a commodity that Lou Richards, alias 'Louie the Lip', has very little of. Louie, my co-host on Channel 9's 'Wide World of Sports — Sunday Edition' and yours truly were looking at the battered, rusty bars of the Sole Bros lion cage along with about 4000 circus fans.

Most of them were school kids with fresh faces and bulging eyes. They had paid good money to be there and it didn't matter that their bums were numb from sitting on the cold, collapsible metal seats, because they were visibly excited.

So too was Louie and myself, but for totally different reasons — Louie had already been to the toilet four times before he entered the ring! It's not that my little mate had a weak bladder, he was genuinely terrified at the thought of entering the lion's cage. To be honest, I wasn't exactly the Rock of Gibraltar either. I'd also managed to sneak in a nervous one before we had to get fair dinkum with the King of the Animal Kingdom.

When our turn to entertain the masses arrived, Lou was dead set shaking in his boots, all 73kg of him. The little bloke kept sinking deeper and deeper into the smelly sawdust as his ankles knocked against each other in perfect harmony with his chattering teeth. The noise was embarrassing!

We were both dressed in 'Dr Livingstone, I presume,' outfits complete with pith helmets, matching Khaki shirts and trousers. Sue from 'wardrobe' at Channel 9 had gone to a lot of trouble in outfitting us. The knee-high boots, for example, had been used in the Aussie film epic — 'Gallipoli.' But I'm not too sure from where she grabbed our bullet-laden gun belts. Louie's oversized belt looked more like the supportive back-brace Dean Lukin wore during his heavyweight gold medal lift in the '84 L.A. Olympics. It even had two very impressive brass buckles to thread through. At first I didn't realise this wasn't purely aesthetic, because he had another belt on underneath this one to hold up his baggy trousers. The other real possibility of course was to pass Louie's salivating tongue through the buckles too — after all Louie the Lip's flapper is in exactly the same proportion as his mouth — XXOS! To complete this otherwise bizarre outfit the former Collingwood captain had continued his fascination for large clothes . . . his shirt sleeves were at least 4 cm too long. I'm sure the little bloke would have preferred the freedom of a sleeveless 'Magpie' guernsey.

On the other hand, the 'Anzac' who proudly marched into battle wearing my boots must have been lean and hungry. I haven't developed the

13

greatest set of calf muscles in the world . . . and after killng time in these cobbler's delights for an hour or so, not much circulation was making it to the ends of my toes — they were cold and numb! The positive side of jamming both feet into an old pair of boots at least two sizes too small was that it took my mind off the unpleasant ordeal ahead.

Lou was still trembling all over when 'beastmaster', Lindsay Perry, cracked his stockman's whip above his head like Indiana Jones in the 'Temple of Doom'. It was great showmanship and he was obviously a man chock full of confidence. For Louie and myself, that caged enclosure symbolised our 'temple of doom'!

The mobile carriage used to transport the lions, was backed up to the ring. Up went the barred door and we were treated to our first glimpse — they were unbelievable! Out they came one after the other. Real snarling, prowling, ferocious-looking lions! I counted four. That was enough! Lou suggested it didn't matter, "'cause there was no way known I'm going in there while they're still roaming around!"

Then I reminded him why we were dressed differently and peering through lots of sets of iron bars. We were shooting a Wide World of Sports 'promo'. The initial concept dreamt up by our producer, Stephen Phillips, was to get an enormous roaring lion to jump through a metal hoop framing a paper sign with the Channel Nine W.W.O.S. identification. As a visual concept, it was a beauty, but in reality it was frightening stuff . . . Thanks Steve. I was beginning to believe there were more than nine dots next to the 9.

By this stage, Lou's face was as grey as his hair, and for once in his life the legendary 'Lip' had nothing cheeky or funny to say. And if I'm not mistaken, he was too busy praying to the big fella in the sky to give anybody the 'Kiss of Death' . . . it's hard to believe but, yes . . . the little fella was on his knees in the damp sawdust. You couldn't blame him because Nero, a 300kg, eight-year-old African lion, appeared to be 'toe-sniffing' in the direction of Lou! He looked like a very hungry lion!

We received a comforting reception from the capacity crowd under the big top when Lindsay, the liontamer, announced our presence and objective. The worst thing that could happen to us, he told the anxious gathering was, "They could be eaten alive if they're not careful!"

The more I thought about it, the worse it got. I felt like a tail-end batsman waiting to get bounced by a manic fastbowler from the Caribbean.

Then a couple of the lionesses appeared upset when our cameraman, Mick Perdy, turned on the floodlights and pointed his lens in their direction. Remember, we still weren't inside the cage!

Finally we could put it off no longer. On cue, we entered the enclosure looking as confident as two guys could who had never even patted a real lion before and never wanted to!

I said to my little multi-media megastar mate: "Let's get this over and done with quickly; grab a hoop so the flaming lion can jump through it and we can get the hell out of here!"

"It's all right for you!" Louie snapped with some of his old fire. "You're only skin and bone (all 95 kg and 193 cm of me) since you went on that diet. . . . . . they'll have a dash at me first! Where are they going to find another me?"

Mind you, that was a pretty good question. They definitely threw the mould away when they cast Lou!

"Anyway!" he stated arrogantly, "Channel 9 can always find another old hasbeen fast bowler or a batsman. They're two bob a dozen!"

I guess he was referring to the Nine cricket commentary team consisting of Richie Benaud, Tony Greig, Ian Chappell, Bill Lawry, Doug Walters, Rodney Marsh and myself!

As I gingerly took up my position between two stools, I could feel the hot sticky breaths of three restless animals tickling the back of my neck — none of them used MacLeans toothpaste for sure — their breath was dreadful!

At this stage the knot in my stomach was becoming unbearable and the lump in my throat had lodged somewhere between my ears. I don't know how Louie was doing beside me but I bet he was pleased to have his oversized trousers tucked in, so there were no tell-tale signs of his nervous condition!

We had positioned the hoop above our heads as directed. That wasn't easy because of Lou's size. Somehow Melbourne's answer to George Burns hung on grimly to the bottom side of the hoop while standing on his tip toes. We were told to hang on tight because if the Lion missed the metal rim he'd be just as likely to knock both of us over and land on top of us. Don't even think about it!

One crack of the whip and around came Nero, a wonderfully fit looking animal with his large black pupils focused only on the hoop. He knew exactly where he was going. Two bounding paces and his front paws reached the top of the stool, quickly followed by his powerful hindquarters. Lou's eyes were now shut tightly in much the same way as a child's — when they don't want to see the growling dog at the end of the street roll up its upper lip to expose its sharp teeth.

But no problems with Nero — straight through the eye diddle diddle. A perfect leap. The cameras were rolling, lights glaring and even the odd flashbulb exploded as he landed on the other stool. Fantastic.

Louie looked at me with a, 'What did I tell ya,' look, out of total relief. The verbal diarrhoea was about to flow. Behind me the big cats were still showing us their stained teeth while clawing at Lindsay who had a chair in one hand and a whip in the other.

Louie was wrong again. The party wasn't quite over. He nearly fainted when our cameraman produced a second hoop. "An insurance shot!" he said. "just in case!"

So back in position for 'take two'. Nero did a lap of honour, flaired his nostrils and away he went. Another direct hit. We just wanted to make a quick exit.

Before we made a move, Nero had completed a 'U-turn' and was heading back towards us. Lindsay smirked at Lou ducking his head, as if appealing for a free kick. At the same time the other lions began running around and around and around us. I was getting edgy and very giddy watching them.

Fortunately Lindsay called them to attention and down they sat, side by side, like big puppies — butter wouldn't melt in their mouth.

Now with everything under control. Louie played up to the crowd. The chirpy little ex-magpie performed a few pirouettes with the bare minimum of finesse. My exit was more of a modest acknowledgement that we were leaving in one piece — just a raising of the right hand.

As the stench of lion droppings filled the big top, we bolted for safety like Laurel and Hardy, "Shut the gate behind you please . . . the lions might get out!" was the parting tongue in cheek remark from the ringmaster. Colour was beginning to flush back into my cheeks. We had done the deed unscathed — one to tell the grandchildren about!

"Did you see them have a swipe at me?" Lou asked. "It was a bit dicey for a while!" he went on.

"Good thing you had me in there to look after you Maxie!"

I thought to myself 'Yeah, Louie . . . . there was no way you were even going near this cage if I didn't first agree to go in with you!'

But then again little blokes are all the same aren't they? Those of you that are under five foot and finished growing will agree with Louie, but that's alright because he always get's it wrong, you only have to follow his footy tipping to know that!

As for aspirations of being lion-tamers, Louie will stick to the Fitzroy Football Club (The Lions) and I'll be content to see Australia whip the pants off the English cricket team. It's got to be easier than watching your life flash before your eyes inside a cage full of lions. Once is certainly enough for me, they can just keep replaying that same old footage!

And no matter how often I look at that footage I keep returning to the same conclusion — Lou is not a pretty sight! Spare a thought for the lions.

I think 'Captain Blood' Jack Dyer, the rough and tough Richmond ruckman was spot on when he told me: "That Lou was so ugly as a kid that his mum used to have to hang the lamb chops around his neck to get their dog to play with him".

Actually on Sunday mornings it's always a pleasure going to work, if you can call sitting down in a chair with Louie and talking sport in front of some of the best sporting pictures in the world at the time, work!

Louie is always vibrant, lively and outrageously funny, but deep down my mate really is like a lovable labrador pup . . . and like the pup, Lou loves being loved. Don't we all?

16

A Touch of the Old Dart

'MY SECOND OF THREE DARTS ALSO FAILED TO GET ANYWHERE NEAR THE DART BOARD — IT HIT A FAN'

Listen here . . . I'm the first bloke to agree with you that it's very frustrating sitting in the air-conditioned loungeroom at home, with the toenails up in the air, phone off the hook, a cold six-pack at your side and just when the live sports telecast gets interesting — they go to a commercial break.

But the cost of a live sporting coverage amounts to almost $3000 a minute — so the money has got to come from somewhere. Hence the commercials!

So as you can see, for just about everyone, except at times the viewer, it's an extremely serious business with heaps of money at stake . . .

In 1985 Dougie Walters and I were used as 'talent', and I use that term loosely, for a Tooheys 2.2 light ale commercial. It turned out to be a lot of fun, depicting yours truly as the world's worst golfer, and at the same time establishing the duo of Walters and Walker . . . hardly Laurel and Hardy, but I bet that pair had humble beginnings too!

A few months later Mojo, the highly successful creative advertising company, insisted that Dougie and I tackle the silver screen again — this time for two new 30-second epic masterpieces, for the same client, Tooheys.

It sounded like a good idea when we first discussed it, but when my bedside phone rang with a wake-up call at 4 a.m. on the first morning of shooting, I wasn't so sure!

At the time, I didn't believe a telephone could make that much noise . . . the reverberating bells were still echoing inside my sensitive skull an hour later!

The Bull and Bush Hotel in Baulkham Hills, Sydney, was the location for our first day's filming. Now even though it was only 5.15 in the morning, where do you think my mate Dougie was? And he has been known to have a drink in his day!

Yes, looking very much at home in the bar . . . cigarette in one hand but a cup of coffee in the other! '

As he said to me: "The day's only a pup Tangles . . . plenty of time for a beer after the sun comes up!" He was spot on with that comment because the next 14 hours were pretty solid going.

While the camera crew, sound team and directors were setting up the scene in the main bar to look as if a local darts competition was in full swing, Doug and I met 'make-up' and 'wardrobe' — two lovely girls named Sally and Sandy.

When they produced our specially-made darts shirts — red, white and blue, in pure silk, I thought . . . strewth, how good is a bloke going to look in this clobber. One look at Dougie and I knew — he looked like an out-of-

17

work jockey but as he said: "The huge blue patch pockets are an ideal size for parking a day's supply of cigarettes." After all Dougie Walters did once smoke 100 cigarettes in 24 hours.

After a few minutes in the make-up chair, Sally had the two of us looking like a couple of seasoned dart players. Although, as the script pointed out, my ability with the feather-tailed missile was to be very ordinary!

In fact the first scene describes exactly that . . . after losing 58 consecutive matches, my first dart hits a timber column almost a metre to the right of the dartboard. And my sarcastic little mate offers me the use of a claw tooth hammer to extract my stray dart! Dougie reckoned my problem was in the elbow!

The action had started — so had the words. Most people outside were struggling with the nightmare of driving a car to work in peak-hour Sydney traffic.

Inside the intimate atmosphere of the Bull and Bush's public bar our biggest problem was to make the room look like it was 9.30 at night.

That was fine . . . it just meant a guy crawled in and out of the set with a 'smoke making machine' a metal cylinder containing some paper to set alight, a spout and a primitive bellows arrangement to expel the smoke.

I'm sure we were burning plastic coated paper early in the shoot because I almost died of smoke inhalation . . . it didn't worry Doug, actually it prompted him to light up a fresh one.

At one stage Dougie came to the rescue of our smoke man by getting down on all fours and proceeding to do the drawback . . . no smoke threaded away from his ears, but I'm sure if I'd asked him, Dougie could have obliged — there's not much the little fella can't do!

So much for the smoke! Just about everyone in the room, including 30-odd extras, had bulging eyeballs and more red lines running across 'em than a city street directory.

It was a pretty tough day for the extras because despite being in a beer commercial they weren't supposed to be drinking in it. Some of them had a beer in their hand as early as 7 a.m. and that same beer was still in each of their sweaty little palms some five hours later — imagine how warm it must have been and no head! Definitely not the kind of beer you die for, is it?

The other problem was to get everyone to act as if they had a few and were enjoying the atmosphere of a big 'darts' night after work — at 7 a.m. in the morning!

Take it from me it wasn't easy. Most people don't get their marbles moving till after 10 a.m. — you know, a cup of coffee with the morning paper syndrome.

The more I got to know our two sharpshooting opponents the more they convinced me they'd played a lot of darts. Both lads spoke with deep English accents and really looked at home with a pint mug in their hands . . . just like in 'the Old Dart'.

18

Through all the action Dougie was never more than an elbow away from the bar — you could say entrenched!

My second of three darts also failed to get anywhere near the dart board — it hit the fan and I mean literally. You should have seen 'em all go for cover. Guys and gals under tables, spreadeagled on the floor and beer spilt everywhere. Absolute pandemonium!

Only one man kept his cool, Dougie — standing at the bar, he didn't spill a drop and he didn't so much as blink an eyelid.

Meanwhile my hostile dart had deflected off the ceiling fan, bounced off the ceiling and lodged firmly in the snout of a huge deer head which happened to be mounted on a wall to my left.

Then down came the mounted deer head, antlers and all . . . Doug is still sipping on his beer but gets time to state: "And . . . that's no bull!" No emotion in his face, eyes slightly squinting, he'd managed to tip the bucket on me again. I guess in the finished product I do look like the world's worst dart player . . . well that's the way it's meant to look.

Doug gets time to state:
"And . . . that's no bull!"

19

I didn't get to see how well Dougie could throw a dart until all the serious talking to the camera had been captured on film and the director was happy.

It's common knowledge — almost folklore in the cricket world — that the great Dougie Walters used to throw darts into the back of the dressing-room doors for bowling practice — it worked too, because this unusual sort of pre-match warm-up, enabled him to dismiss 49 batsmen at Test level . . . and that's no bull!

Amazingly the first dart he did fire at the dart board hit the bull's eye . . . as if he needed any confidence, that was it, back to the bar for another beer.

"You'll need to do better than Robin Hood to beat that, Tangles!" he said smugly.

As usual he was right . . . never more at home having a chat and a smoke over a beer, discussing cricket, card tricks, jacking up a game of snooker or taking the mickey out of me.

For the record, this commercial took a day and a half to shoot! After all it wasn't that easy to get my second dart to bounce off the revolving ceiling fan and then lob precisely on the moose's head. There is no way known Doug could achieve that degree of skill!

So next time you see a commercial you hate or maybe it just irritates you, appreciate the time and effort it took to look that bad!

Bath Time was Never Like This

'I AGREED TO DEMONSTRATE HOW EASY IT WAS TO BATH WITH A FRIEND'

All in a day's work I suppose! I was standing alone in an old vacant church, with five bikini-clad young women. The rain was pelting down outside and the cold damp sand was abrasive between my not-so-pretty toes.

Yes, there I was stranded on a 'desert island' with not just one lovely body to keep me company but five of 'em! The mind boggles doesn't it — a dream come true! Nola, Olga, Jenny, Sandy and Sandy.

But the mere fact that we were gathered under a wonderfully ornate timber church ceiling kept my mind holy — above the devious — and focusing tightly on the day ahead. Not on the beach belles!

The occasion was the shooting of an in-house corporate video for the Beautyware Bath people. What a novel way to show off their bathware — in a church, on a beach, and using five bathing beauties, plus yours truly as decoration.

Truckloads of sand had been dumped inside the beautiful old sandstone building to artificially create our beach front. A very talented artist had spent many days on canvas to provide the set with a horizon fit for a lush tropical paradise . . . and that's what it was shaping up to be. I couldn't wait!

It was 7.30 a.m., the atmosphere was one of anticipation, the air was icy cold and several small strip heaters were the focus of much popularity by the girls.

The girls kept putting off the inevitable — a walk past the camera and director. I really felt for them . . . it was a truly bracing experience, and showed. You'd reckon these girls would have ironed their bikini tops! But several didn't — the peg marks were quite visible!

Meanwhile, Trish, the make-up lady, was assessing just how much paint was needed to turn me into a bronzed life-saver.

I've never contemplated the possibility of being hand-painted in mission brown — and by a lady, too! Apart from the insides of my delicate thighs being a bit sensitive to the paint brush, it worked. For the first time in my life I could honestly say I was brown — though it wasn't the sort of weather to hang around half-naked waiting for wet paint to dry on my goose-pimpled body.

And the thought of plunging bottom first into any one of the five sunken bath tubs was hardly inviting . . . the odds on the water in the baths staying warm were very slim.

Once the sequence of filming was nutted out by the director, it was time to get fair dinkum. I sat comfortably in a cane beach chair, sun glasses gently perched on my nose and cocktail drink locked into my left hand, while the girls paraded a series of body hugging costumes in various colors until everyone was happy. I was happy with them all.

For the moment I was comparatively covered up with my World War II style khaki shorts and floral shirt . . . my turn would come soon enough.

The first to take a deep breath was Nola, a tall, slim brunette with a high-jumper's body. She ever so slowly lowered the bottom half of her teeny weeny red bikini into an old fashioned gentleman's bath, until the plimsol line was well above her navel. A breathtaking experience! She was then asked to lay back in the beautiful old four-legged, cast-iron container. Easier said than done!

The shiny enamelled surface of the bath was like a sheet of ice. How could she smile through clenched teeth?

Then her bottom was having trouble gripping the slippery bottom of the bath and by the time she'd glamorously finished soaping up her arms and legs, Nola had slid about half way down into the bath . . .

All the flexing of the muscles in her buttocks was not going to be sufficient to keep her upright and smiling! More bubbles, more hot water and an old house brick wrapped in a hand towel solved the problem!

Nola now had a foothold and looked very relaxed and much at home in the water which by this time was getting colder by the minute!

After several 'takes' the girl in the red bikini leapt out of the tub, snuggled up in a huge towel and positioned herself appropriately in front of the strip-heater.

At this stage it was only 9 a.m. and all I'd done was sit in my deck chair and enjoy what was happening.

Since the other bathtubs were buried creatively into the beach-head in a very temporary manner, there was no waste pipe fitted to the plug holes. Thus there was no quick way of emptying the water other than the same way it entered the bath — in a bucket. So throughout the day hundreds of buckets of hot and cold water were moved around our desert island paradise.

One of the baths was big enough for two . . . so of course I agreed to demonstrate how easy it was to bath with a friend! I even managed to get my back scrubbed . . . and just when the scene was getting interesting and I was getting very clean, the director said he'd got enough pictures to satisfy the client. Gee, some blokes have got no sense of timing!

It was probably just as well because I'd been in the water a long time and my skin was beginning to crinkle up!

Then, like a creature from the Black Lagoon, Sandy, dressed in a one piece suit bobbed up from the bottom of the adjoining bath an arms length away.

Now I should mention that all five models were knockouts, it's just that Sandy in pink was a bit bigger than the remaining quadrella. All four were winners whichever way I looked at them.

Like a carefree playful whale — a huge fountain of water shot straight up. Yes, Sandy had the lot — face mask and snorkel. It looked hilarious! As the script suggested Sandy had mischief on her mind and I had a fair idea of the plot at this stage!

It wasn't going to work out as expected — Maxie, plus four beauties. Just Sandy and Maxie, if the one-piece terror had anything to do with it.

Anyway I didn't give up hope. I thought maybe the directors might lose the plot and my suggestion of a different ending would be more appropriate, but no such luck.

Several pages of foolscap dialogue later, I still didn't look like winning one of the beauties — everytime I had a bit of a chance the never-say-die Sandy was looming over my shoulder.

Just when the storyline changed and seemed to be running my way, up bobbed the bigger Sandy again, complete with an enormous pink flower protruding above her left ear and a tropical punch cocktail in her hand.

Jenny had sand in her face and I must say the amount of sediment and sand on the bottom of my bath made sitting down a bit like sliding up and down on a piece of grade nine sandpaper.

As well as the persistent Sandy, I had to contend with my rubber ducks . . . they reminded me of Kim Hughes and Greg Chappell a few summers back.

Several shampoos later it was my turn to pamper the other Sandy — she made Tarzan's Jane look average. And after four big lathers I bet her hair has never been cleaner.

Now Olga — almost six-foot of great bodyline added a new dimension to plain blue bikinis. But despite my fantasies of ending up with the quartet of bronze beauties . . . no such luck!

Sandy saw to that . . . like the Royal Canadian Mounted Police who always get their man — so did Sandy!

Ready to show the world

'DOUGIE BATTED FOR HALF AN HOUR AS BUDDING FAST BOWLERS LINED UP FOR A CRACK AT HIM'

It was 3 o'clock in the morning. Two young boys sat on the edge of their dormitory beds, feet barely touching the floor. Inside their tummies huge butterflies danced up and down . . .

The occasion was the final day of the live-in Max Walker Cricket Camp held at the famous Assumption College, Kilmore, Victoria in February, 1986.

Their wide-eyed reply was brief and to the point: "How long till the game starts?"

Today they would be playing a cricket match . . . for many youngsters it would be the first time they had ever played in an official cricket match. A big step forward!

It was a real pleasure to witness the pride each of these budding cricketers had in their own ability . . . they wanted to show the world they could play the game! And that alone was a wonderfully healthy attitude to have.

Each of these little 'champions' had his bat gently resting on the floor. They weren't going to waste any time either, for both were fully dressed in their all-white cricket gear, glowing in the dark.

When questioned by the housemaster on duty that night as to what they were doing, their wide-eyed reply was brief and to the point. "How long till the game starts? It was almost enough to make a grown man cry with joy.

Yet today we see our Test players using former greats like Dennis Lillee and Rod Marsh to get them motivated. Surely a Test cricketer doesn't need another person to tell him he should be giving his super best when representing Australia!

The beautiful truth is that all these juniors want to play Test cricket . . . and I reckon they all dream about striding to the wicket at the MCG just about every night they put their weary little bodies down to rest after a solid day's cricket.

Every camp has its characters and this year was no different. In all we had three camps —two at Kilmore and the third at Launceston. The boys travelled far and wide to improve their game.

In fact one young fella named Rhys became the darling of all the coaches. He had been holidaying in England with his parents and come straight from Tullamarine airport to Kilmore . . . no jet-lag with Rhys.

The nine-year-old 'Bradman' was so small he commanded a great deal of respect from his peers. Add his cheery nature and bright beaming smile and the diminutive little Aussie had his mates eating out of the palm of his hand.

One boy came all the way from India to join the camp. It didn't take long for the lads to nickname him 'Kapil Dev' . . . and what's more he loved being identified with his native hero.

Then there was 'an individual' named Mark Jackson — he even had the prickly, crew-cut hair-do. You'd never guess, he was called 'Jacko'.

Another kid they called 'Rambo' because he wore the same jungle greens and black track-suit trousers for four days.

They were quite an incredible bunch. At shower time they all became very scarce — some of the 9-10 year olds needed an operation to get their clothes off. In fact some of them used to hide in the cupboards and under the beds.

And then there was 'The Professor' who came back to us for the second year . . . he knew everything. He just wouldn't shut up — like a tape recorder with a new set of batteries.

On the first morning he said, "Remember me? I'm the fellow who bowled two balls into the nets last year and got a wicket with each ball!" How could I forget.

One kid used his protector (box) when he was bowling because his follow through arm usually ended up between his legs. He had a very awkward action — so much so that we nicknamed him 'Richard Hadlee'.

The coaches were the key to the camp's success. Each and every one of them was of the highest possible order and a great communicator. But they also copped some flak from the boys.

Kerry O'Keeffe, former Australian and NSW leg spinner received a beauty from young Jeremy Stebbings. He said, "I bet you don't know what that 'brain sucker' is doing on your head?" Kerry didn't have a clue. The kid gave him a rather cutting answer, "Going hungry!"

Then we had everybody's favorite and one of the greatest players ever to pull on a boot for Australia, Doug Walters.

One night Dougie batted for half an hour as budding fast bowlers lined up for a crack at him. Much in the mould of Sir Donald Bradman, Dougie didn't let 'em down. He kept middling the ball beautifully. One straight drive cleared the sight screen 60 metres away . . .

Then came the acid tongue of Kerry O'Keeffe trying to discipline one wayward leg-spinner.

"That's the worst ball I've ever seen bowled in my life!" he screamed as the ball landed 20 metres to the left of where it ought to have. "I think you should go and lock yourself in the toilet for half an hour and think about it!"

There was never a dull moment, even at night. One of our night staff, discovered a sleep-walker . . . he had no alternative but to wake him up because he didn't have his name tag on and he didn't know where the poor kid came from.

Test player Simon O'Donnell used the three camps to overcome an injured hip. It's the same injury which side-lined him after the Australia v. New Zealand Test match at the SCG in December, 1985. He was a huge hit with the group — so were our two West Indian coaches.

Ken Benjamin, a fast bowler from the island of Antigua, soon became a bit hit with his outgoing nature. He was in Australia on an education scholarship along with Guyanese batsman and off-spinner Carl Hooper. Hooper won rave revues for his performances in the 1985 West Indies domestic season.

At night there was plenty of entertainment. During the screening of the Centenary Test film in Launceston the roof almost came off the theatre when 220 schoolboys chanted, "Lill-ee, Lill-ee, Lill-ee," as the champion fast bowler took apart the Englishmen in March 1977. Dennis Lillee took 11 wickets for the match — they had plenty to shout about.

There was not much need for punishment throughout the 12 days of coaching . . . but Brother Pius at Assumption College had a good method of discipline! One night at 11.30 p.m. two boys had to do four laps of the oval in the rain and in the dark, on separate ovals — a bit scary!

The young man who got my courage award was Jason. Jason had a physical disability that would have stopped a lot of boys participating — he only had the use of his left side.

He even bowled off a lengthy run, by dragging himself along, just to be like the other boys. We cut his run down and within a couple of days I was amazed at his improvement . . . the way the ball left his hand, seam vertical. I was really proud of him.

When he batted in the nets he quietly asked one of the coaches if the boys would mind not bowling so fast at him — they didn't.

When Jason played his match on the fourth day his mates clapped him all the way out to bat . . . he made a one-handed four which was a gutsy effort . . . his mates clapped him all the way off.

He acknowledged the applause by quietly stating, "It was an easy hundred boys"!

There are so many stories of humour, courage and sadness amongst the 750 odd boys we shared some time with.

Sure there were some tearful beginnings as is always the case when a youngster leaves his parents behind for the first time — a painful necessary learning experience.

Michael took his stuffed dog to bed with him, another had the Sesame Street phone book on the window-sill.

With all those mixed emotions thrown in it was great to hand them all a certificate of proficiency at our wonderful game — just to see them smile was a priceless gift.

It was also wonderful on the final day in Kilmore to over hear two young mates saying to each other, "I'll write you a letter"!

For many it was a chance to make their first real friend outside of family and school — they shared so much under the name of cricket.

We never stop learning about the game — if you do, it's time to give it away!

Glutton for punishment

'HE ONCE ATE 14 MEAT PIES AND 19 SAVELOYS — WITHOUT SAUCE'

It was hard to believe that anyone could possibly stuff at least a dozen fresh prawns into their mouth all at once! But I saw it with my own eyes . . . in the person of a fragile, little old lady dressed in a black and white pom-pom hat, black and white cardigan and black knitted dress.

And to top off her outfit she was wearing a pair of blue and white runners with no socks — hardly dressed to kill, eh?

Nevertheless, she was very intent on winning the prawn eating competition that I'd somehow got myself involved in.

My primary reason for being in Gladstone, Queensland, during Easter 1986 was for a single wicket contest, and certainly not to make a glutton of myself in public.

There I was, along with seven other hungry characters, standing around an old timber trestle. In front of each of us was placed a huge plastic bag of medium-sized prawns . . . the pile must have been a foot high. That's a lot of prawns, so the first prize of 40 kilos of fresh prawns was the last thing I needed!

Everyone was poised, forearms tensed ready for a standing start, especially the tiny old lady with the big appetite and wrinkled face opposite me.

The atmosphere was electric, the starter's gun punctured the air and was followed by the sickening sound of prawn munchers! There really is no other sound quite like the simultaneous crunching of prawn shells! Although, one of the contestants decided to shell them and stockpile until there was a sufficient number to cram into the mouth for one huge gulp — not a pretty sight!

The pace was hectic — both skill and technique was necessary to keep up with the leaders. A muscular, tattooed dude, and the little old lady were neck and neck — or should I say mouthful and mouthful.

The man with the tattoos on his arm was a 'peel and stockpiler' . . . three easy actions. Head off, tail off, then shell the rest.

On the other hand, the skinny little woman with the rubbery face had very little class . . . in they went, heads, tails and whatever else, sometimes 12 at a time. Incredible.

My stomach squirmed, as she continually chomped away like a pelican swallowing a huge fish. Never once did that tell-tale lump in her throat express itself in a painful expression. Her eyes remained fixed on the diminishing pile of pink prawns.

I had barely made in-roads into my quota of prawns when the contest was all over. A muscle-bound sailor standing opposite me signalled he had finished by raising his right hand above his head — he half-smiled through clenched teeth, saliva and prawn shell dribbling from the corner of his mouth. It was easy to see he'd made a complete guts of himself.

Just seconds later a shout of relief as the black and white lady punched the sky like Rocky's grandmother.

She was very outspoken at the result, claiming victory was hers, on the grounds that she had eaten the shell and heads whereas the other guy hadn't. The final result stood, but she didn't leave empty handed — the organisers gave her 20 kilos for a very gutsy effort!

Meanwhile cricketers Glenn Trimble, Peter Clifford and myself performed like novices and were still eating prawns out of a plastic bag an hour later.

27

My heart and stomach weren't really in this little episode, but don't get me wrong I used to be pretty good on the tooth! So too did my dad!

He once ate 14 meat pies and 19 saveloys, without sauce, to win a local football pre-night eating competition, in Tasmania. In fact, he won by three savs, after his main rival had filed to keep his tally intact — I'm told he left the changerooms in search of fresh air, in a big hurry and looked a trifle green around the gills when he came back.

My only success at over-indulging came to me quite by chance during the 1973 Australian cricket tour of the Caribbean.

We'd just spent a few weeks in Guyana and apart from the cricket, it was a pretty depressing place to be. Everywhere we looked poverty confronted us. So too did the politics of the country.

On top of all this the food wasn't too flash either. A steady diet of chicken ranging in color from white to green was consistently fed to us. So too was the alternative — curried goat, fried rice and 25 different varieties of blowflies, some of 'em big buggers too.

But, much to our relief, our next venue was the beautiful island paradise of Tobago. Now here food was not a problem, nothing was a problem.

We couldn't believe the food . . . it was the ideal venue for an eating competition.

Jeff Hammond the South Australian fast bowler with a build like a walking coat-hanger, reckoned he was a better 'fang-man' than me. I accepted the challenge with a great deal of pleasure.

It just happened that the evening meal on our first night in Tobago was a smorgasbord — you beauty! It was virtually 10 square metres piled high with every food conceivable — salads, hot dishes, cold meats and a magnificent assortment of sweets, which I love.

After getting through two plates each containing two corn on the cobs, two huge slices of beef, two potatoes wrapped in silver foil with a few peas, we tackled the cold collations with a great deal of vigor.

Almost an hour of absolutely identical eating had passed when I suggested we tackle the sweets — my strong point!

We began by downing three pastry tarts and three colorful jellies. I must admit I was beginning to feel the pinch as my belly was stretched to its limit!

Next the tall black waiter tempted the two of us with the biggest banana splits I've ever seen. He said, "Compliments of the chef." The word had spread to the kitchen that we were nearing the business end of the 'meal'.

The bananas must have been 12 inches long, enclosing three scoops of ice-cream and with strawberry topping and nuts . . . absolutely delicious. My opponents Jeff was beginning to struggle — I could see it in his eyes.

Somehow I emptied my plate of fruit and ice-cream . . . then applied some old-fashioned gamesmanship. I grabbed another six jellies and placed them on the table in front of Jeff.

His reaction was predictable — almost physically sick and he accepted

the offer of a drink. Coffee was the medium-pacer's choice, mine was lemon tea.

I said, "Three more jellies each mate then we'll get fair dinkum!" It worked.

The coffee swilled around in his mouth and refused to dive down to the depths of his stomach. The level remained constant, at about gum-level, as he tried to combine a smile and a burp. I polished off one lone jelly and my opponent conceded . . . I was definitely bluffing. One more jelly and my game would have been over too.

Chaos on the Lake

'MY WHOLE BODY VIBRATED AS THE REAR OF THE BOAT BURIED ITSELF'

The louder the six litre Chevrolet engine barked, the faster my heart began. We were travelling at 160 kmh across the calm surface of the Albert Park Lake in Melbourne.

I had just accepted an offer to go for a quick spin around the lake in *Kaos* — one of this country's most consistent K-class circuit race boats. The driver of the sleek looking boat was Australia's leading unlimited blown displacement boat racer, Peter Smith.

What an exhilarating experience! There I was, 'Tanglefoot', in all my glory, a tangle of arms and legs wedged backwards into where a passenger's seat ought to have been.

As we drifted clear of the grotty concrete lake edge and loading ramp, I still couldn't convince myself that it was a good idea. My imagination kept doubting my decision with graphic images of power boats flipping over and exploding in mid air.

Basically the K-class blown displacement boats are souped up ski-boats but it should be mentioned that these craft can travel at about 200 kmh. Obviously if you're intending to spend a lot of time racing these power-house machines then a good insurance policy is a must.

Pete turned the key to start the fuel injected engine — and my whole body vibrated as the rear of the boat buried itself into a trench of foaming water. The nose was angled steeply towards the treetops and there was no question that from here on in it was a matter of hanging on tight!

It was tough enough sitting backwards but I was copping the G-forces in reverse. With every surge of power the boat lunged forward and my head was wedged between my legs, so great was the force.

Yes, it was rodeo time. It felt like we were only hitting the tops of waves every 20 metres or so. Not having either a seat or suspension made the journey a real bone crusher.

But wow, what a buzz. Looking to where we'd come from, instead of where we were going was great. With a huge draught tearing away at the back of my neck, it was breathtaking stuff!

Peter suggested I spin my head around to view the scenery up front, but somehow the ball bearings in my neck wouldn't allow me to complete a 360-degree turn! Anyway I did manage to half turn, only to find it almost impossible to keep my eyes open. And breathing air entering one's mouth at that pace was something else!

As we manoeuvred around the first marker buoy I was asked to hang on. . . my overhanging left elbow was only millimetres from the water.

I learnt that the more boat the driver can keep out of the water, the faster they go. And at the same time this makes them more difficult to steer accurately. Peter was only too pleased to let me feel the rear slip and slide, and at that pace it was a bit hairy. Imagine being in among a few other crazy drivers, all wanting to be the fastest men in the water. All I can say is good luck!

But for me, I couldn't have been in better hands because Peter Smith was the 1985 national unlimited blown displacement boat racing champion. His career spans 17 years and it is Pete who's been given the credit for pioneering the sport of blown displacement racing.

During his competitive days behind the wheel of various boats only once has he had a bad accident and Peter assures me he's only lost one boat. Not a bad record! Maybe it was this sort of comment that gave me the confidence to accept his offer of a test session on the lake.

But gee, I was pretty pleased to get my feet back on the ground, yet grateful for the chance to share a lap or two with our Aussie champ.

I definitely felt much more at home behind the microphone chatting about his expedition into the 'big time' — K-class racing in the U.S.

Peter unfortunately suffered a similar fate to the legendary Alan Bond of America's Cup fame — every time he blitzed the opposition they changed the rules or declared his boat *Kaos* illegal, even though it had been scrutineered and passed prior to the start of events contested.

The following item appeared in the *National Boat News,* USA, November, 1985, "Aussie K-racer Pete Smith came to the U.S. looking for competition. He's going home with a tainted view of racing, American style. Is he an uncontrollable wild man on the racecourse, or did he get a crash course in K-racing politics?'"

For Pete Smith the opportunity to go to America and race against the best drivers over there was something he'd been planning to do for many years, but instead of being a wonderful enriching experience of competition racing, it turned sour!

Did the Americans take *Kaos* from downunder too lightly? Was that the problem? "I think at first they looked at the boat because they had never seen anything like it. Sure they've got boats that are comparable — their own injected super-charged boats — but the whole design of *Kaos* is different," Peter said.

"And it was the Australian design that killed 'em!. They looked at it, shook their heads and laughed. But when it showed them the back of it, they soon stopped laughing!"

Eventually this 'new' design as well as Pete Smith's courage proved too much for the other drivers and the American authorities to handle — they don't like losing, particularly to an outsider in a modified ski boat.

What a pity the Americans were not prepared to back their boats' raw racing talent, and courage against Pete Smith and his boat *Kaos* without the security and comfort of being able to make their own rules.

Still, thanks for the ride, Pete!

Catching Butterflies for a Living

'WITH TV COSTING THOUSANDS OF DOLLARS A MINUTE, A SURGE OF ADRENALIN IS UNLEASHED'

You don't have to be a sporting person to suffer from the equivalent of match nerves or butterflies in the tummy. It happens to most of us at some stage or other as we ponder the possibilities or outcome of a future event . . . it doesn't even have to be a contest.

I'm sure anyone who has ever sat anxiously waiting for his turn to speak at a gathering of people can relate to having a gut-wrenching sensation in the stomach, and eyes locked into a mad stare at the lonely lectern — the only object on the stage that will ultimately be between yourself and them!

It might be comforting to know that even a great performer like Barry Humphries goes through terrible periods of pre-night nerves!

These nervous conditions take on many forms, particularly at sporting events!

For example, I'm told that the former great Test cricketer Norman O'Neill used to dry-retch and occasionally even vomit, before entering the arena to bat for his country. Former Test batsman, Rick Darling suffered the same sort of pre-match ordeal.

My mate Dougie Walters was the direct opposite ... he'd keep one eye on the game and the other on a game of cards — usually patience. All the time puffing away at a comforting ciggy.

Footballers generally treasure the solitude of the rub-down table. Heaven is an oily towel draped over a player's head while the steel-like fingers of the masseur fine tune the body.

It is not difficult to totally relax under these conditions. And that is the key to the whole exercise — to be able to control that super-charged nervous energy so that it can be put to use during the competition or performance.

To win at the L.A. Olympics in 1984, big Dean Lukin, the tuna fisherman from Port Lincoln, had to harness more positive energy than he had ever done before.

Imagine how the big fella must have felt before his final lift? Martinez, the super heavyweight lifter from the U.S., virtually had the medal in his keeping.

Dean Lukin had to lift more than he'd ever held above his head ... no good getting nervous, knowing that millions of Australians would witness his attempt on the small screen back home in Australia. He had to use all that anxiety, apprehension and anticipation to his advantage.

It's history now that he drew one last deep breath, and addressed the bar. With vibrating legs and a purple, distorted face identifying his huge effort, he did it. Gold to Australia!

Yes, leave nothing to chance and everything will fall into place. That's fine if you're in a head to head confrontation and you're responsible for your own destiny. But take something like television where the presenter's performance only goes to air after many behind the scenes people do their jobs ... from the camera-man, sound technician, producer, director and plenty more.

That's when the old saying 'trust 'em' really becomes apparent ... to get a perfect score everyone has to be spot on.

There is nothing quite like sitting at a news desk at GTV-9, Melbourne waiting for the red light on camera 3 to light up and the floor manager to signal 'go' by dropping his arm.

Almost as difficult and nerve racking as doing a 'live-cross' — the terminology for an on location report.

Imagine how the big fella must have felt before his final lift?

For example, Brian Naylor might interrupt the news to cross to yours truly at the SCG at stumps on the day's play in a Test match.

This really is the blind leading the blind, not to mention the lads on the hill in the background trying to get into the act with a cheerio to mum!

Here, the only message is, 'Speak for 45 seconds when the producer standing next to the tripod counts you in' . . . 5, 4, 3, 2, 1 — ACTION!

With 'off the cuff' dialogue, it's almost impossible to know how long you've been speaking yet you keep talking. Millions of viewers are trying to make sense of what you're saying.

Then just when there's a change of direction with a new sentence, the producer gives you the wind up signal — a rotation anti-clockwise of the index finger . . . the heart feels heavier . . . what will I do?

I can't pull out mid-sentence and with television costing thousands of dollars per minute, a surge of adrenalin is unleashed deep inside . . . don't let the nerves get the better of you now Maxie . . . think of something appropriate to finish on — but quickly! Suddenly it's all over. "Back to you Brian!"

Someone says, "Well played mate!" I feel okay again — the butterflies disappear till the next time. All I can say at this stage, as someone who constantly lives with a bellyfull of butterflies, is be well-prepared, do your homework, practise hard and believe in yourself and more times than not you will get what is required — a straight line of magnificently colored butterflies!

Chapter Two

MORE MIRTH FROM THE GREAT GAME

Mallett fell in . . . and let out a curse as it exploded.

The Team Jester gets his
'THERE WAS NOTHING SUBTLE ABOUT HIS HUMOUR'

Team spirit is very important. When Clive Lloyd took over as skipper to lead one of the best teams there has been, this real team feeling was evident, and I think it is the same sort of thing I was lucky enough to know in the Australian side in the 1970s.

In those days we had a bloke named Doug Walters who was a prankster, a shrewd card player, a cigarette smoker and a drinker. He was a very important player on the field, but an equally important ingredient to the team's success off the field.

There are countless stories about Dougie, and perhaps a few would explain the sort of fun and inspiration he injected into the team.

I had the fortune, or perhaps misfortune, to room with him on one tour and I quickly discovered what sort of bloke he was.

Dougie rarely slept. He could slip into the room about 4 a.m. I pretended that I was sleeping, and would hear him zip the top off a can and see the glow of a cigarette light the room.

Even at that time of the morning he would declare: "Gee, I really needed that."

The next day when he would wield his bat in a great innings, you got to appreciate how extraordinary a player he was.

There was nothing subtle about his humour. He was a blatant practical joker who searched trick shops throughout the world in a bid to find new ways of trapping players.

During the Melbourne Test against England in 1974-75 he really fixed up Ashley Mallett, who was petrified by any sort of creepy-crawly.

Walters was fielding at mid-off when Mallett was bowling. Dougie attached gum to the ball, then added a plastic tarantula which he slipped from his hip pocket.

He tossed the ball, with imitation spider, to Mallett, who nearly had a heart-attack when he caught it. In front of the huge crowd, Mallett cried out and drop-kicked the ball to the Punt Road end of the ground.

Everyone thought it was marvellous, except Mallett, and it relieved a lot of tension in the middle of a tight session of play.

Walters wasn't bad with the cigarettes either. As he worked for a cigarette firm, he began to become weary of Mallett and Rod Marsh pinching his fags.

So he brought a packet of exploding cigarettes and, on a wet day at Lord's in 1975, waited for one of the culprits to walk up and take one without asking.

Mallett fell in, walked to the balcony, lit the fag, and let out a curse as it exploded and blackened his face.

Marshie was writing home at the time, and his look was pretty dark when that was interrupted by the exploding fag and he had to go to the washroom to clean his face.

Dougie's fags were his own after that.

But I reckon his best trick was the new pound note attached to the end of a nylon fishing line.

He had a little coil spring in the palm of his hand and whenever anyone went to pick up the quid, Dougie would press the gadget and the note would spring back into his hand.

One day he really fixed up Derek Underwood in the English dressing-rooms. He waited until Derek was only a few centimetres from the note when he pressed the gadget, and everyone in the room rolled with laughter. An embarrassed Underwood tried to explain that he knew it belonged to Dougie and that he was merely trying to return it!

But like any prankster, Dougie met his match. He placed the quid in the bar and was waiting for someone to try to pick it up when a paper boy came in trying to sell his wares.

The little nipper saw the note and immediately stamped his foot on it, snapping the line. The kid picked up the money, stuffed it in his pocket and waltzed out of the bar as Dougie stood there dumbfounded.

Doug was very popular with everyone — his team-mates, his opponents and fans around the world.

I can remember once when we were in England, at Leeds in 1977, and I was his tick-tack. Before play Dougie had three bets on the races and he wanted to know how they were faring.

When the first horse bobbed up at 7-1, I yelled out with glee and everyone near the fine-leg fence knew exactly what I was shouting about.

Dougie strutted around for a bit and after a while all the fans knew what he had backed in the next two events. I have no idea how that happened.

Anyway, the next two nags had amazing support from the locals, and when they duly won, Dougie was the toast of the outer.

And all this on the day when Geoff Boycott was scoring his 100th century in his 100th Test at his home ground.

There are hundreds of Walters stories, and it just goes to show what a character he was around the world in the era of a great Australian side.

But importantly for any cricketer, he was an outstanding player. He scored a century in a session on three occasions, and the most memorable was when he hit a six off the last ball of the day from Bob Willis against England in Perth in 1974.

He predicted the milestone to skipper Ian Chappell. Chappell ordered all of us into the shower and left an empty room when Dougie returned in triumph.

After a few minutes, Chappelli stormed out and began criticising Dougie for getting out off the last ball, and it took some time for Dougie to explain that he wasn't out and that in fact he had, as predicted, scored a century in a session.

Eventually everybody broke out in laughter and ran out of the shower to congratulate Dougie.

That's the sort of camaraderie which helped make that side so good, and Walters was the key.

Wired for Expletives

'DENNIS HAD TWO SETS OF VALUES WHEN HE PLAYED CRICKET . . .'

To the average 'Norm' sitting in his lounge room, can of beer in the one hand, cigarette in the other and both feet up on a well-stocked esky, the game of cricket has not been the same since microphones were inserted into the base of middle stumps in 1978.

It added a new 'realism' to television cricket . . . bats nervously tapping on the ground, the sounds of heavily sprigged bowling boots gaining momentum before the delivery stride, the metal toe-cap dragged across the worn pitch next door to the stumps . . . and bellows of "Owzat!"

The first unforgettable, experimental 'sound check' was under lights at the Sydney Cricket Ground. Everyone had their fingers crossed, apart from the members of the Rest of the World X1 and Australian teams. For the most part they were unaware of the impact this new feature was to have on their future behaviour.

Late in the match, Dennis Lillee was batting against the tall blonde fast bowler, Garth La Roux. The South African-born quick was built like a Greek God and had a passion for striking terror into the minds of batsmen and you couldn't help but notice him.

Now, to be fairly honest, Dennis Lillee was perhaps the greatest fast bowler, but as a batsman he was never completely happy about facing anything shorter than a half volley. In fact Dennis had two sets of values when he played cricket — one for when he batted and the other for when he bowled!

I was at the non-strikers end, the best place to be when bowlers of real pace are operating and it was easy to see that big 'Conan' had done his homework on one DK Lillee. He charged in like a steam train out of control — a magnificent sight if you haven't got the bat in your hand.

Unfortunately for Dennis, he did have the bat in his hand and the self-doubt clearly showed in his eyes from where I was standing.

The delivery was fast alright, I could tell that by the fast bowler's grunt as he expelled every last bit of air from his lungs in the final delivery stride.

Adrenalin no doubt was starting to flow through some of the not-so-athletic bodies in front of TV sets as the fearsome sound and image of the Rest of the World 'super quick' filled the screen. I bet the next move was for them to duck, just as the ball was released.

The Aussie tailender had similar thoughts. But like most express bowlers, Garth Le Roux lacked the consistent accuracy of a clear-headed and uncomplicated medium pacer like myself! He unkindly let one go off a very fullish length which took my team-mate by complete surprise. On the full, the white leather 'bullet' struck Dennis on the fleshy inside part of the thigh, just above the pad. The look on the face of my partner said it all . . . SHOCK, HORROR, PAIN! Then came a glare of, 'You'll get yours pal!!!'

For more than a decade, the Dennis Lillee glare did its work, but it was not enough for Dennis . . . it was always backed up with a volley of adjectives. This evening was no exception! Only that the roles were reversed.

What he didn't realise, was that every word he uttered after getting La Roux's 'doodle big' (hand to hip delivery) was being picked up and broadcast to every TV set in the country. Even if the sound wasn't turned up, the viewer wouldn't have had to be a great 'lip-reader' to work out what he was saying. I got the wash of this earbash just standing at the other end. I was embarrassed!

For Channel 9 television magnate and World Series Cricket entrepreneur of the time, Kerry Packer, it was also a moment of high drama. The switchboards of Channel 9 stations around Australia began to light up like Christmas trees with complaints. There was no alternative while the volatile Dennis Lillee was at the crease but to shut down the microphones. As Kerry Packer said to the great bowler, not so great batsman after play, "What's the bloody good of having microphones in the stumps if I'm too scared to turn 'em on!"

The direct result of that innovation was firstly, players were made more aware of what they said and secondly, the microphones were made less sensitive.

There were plenty of other light moments during that pioneering season of cricket. I remember when one of the sound technicians responsible for bringing the armchair enthusiasts that 'extra dimension' came to filling out his 'claimable expenses' form. One gross of the finest quality condoms was the claim. Of course, it was immediately knocked back! The response from the 'dollar scorers' in the accounts branch was something along the lines of, "We don't mind letting you get away with the odd free lunch, but subsidising your excessive sex-life is definitely out of the question!"

It was a genuine claim and later accepted when the 'sound tech' explained that there was a problem of keeping the very expensive piece of equipment dry when rain interrupted play. Before deciding to pull on a condom, everything from 'glad wrap' to plastic bags were tried, but it seemed nothing quite fitted over the middle stump as snuggly and effectively as a good old fashioned condom.

Almost a decade passed before circumstances made it possible to take the next step forward in bringing the sounds of cricket to the television viewer: the players themselves were wired for sound!

The chosen ones, including yours truly, were all years older, less athletic and a bit rustier, nonetheless each and every one of us still fancied ourselves a bit. Call it ego or just plain good ol' Aussie pride . . . we were going to give 'em heaps, God willing.

Yes, it was England v Australia — an exact replay of the original centenary clash. Only English wicketkeeper Alan Knott was unable to play in the charity match. A capacity crowd of 20,000 plus had swelled the WACA ground in Perth and many youngsters in attendance hadn't even been born when these two sides clashed initially in one of the finest Test matches ever played between the traditional rivals.

There were a few questions that had to be asked before the match went ahead. Would anyone turn up to watch us old 'has beens' go through the motions more than a decade later? Would a replay, even the condensed version of 50 overs a side, detract from the original game? What about the quality of cricket? Would we all make fools of ourselves? Do old cricketers never die and do they just grow old gracefully?

One thing for sure is that the ageing process is more sympathetic to batsmen than it is for bowlers, especially 'quicks'. Of course longevity in the game is not something that fast bowlers spend a lot of time thinking about. On average, The Englishmen were five years older than the Australian line-up and it certainly showed in the colour of their greying hair! Mind you, without mentioning any names, there were a few of our lads who were having trouble keeping a good thatch on their head.

In the dressing room before this first of three match series, nothing much had changed. Doug Walters was doing his usual warm up for a stint at bowling by firing a dozen darts into the dart board. Still dressed in his civies, Dougie then casually settled into a characteristic pre-match game of cards with talented all-rounder cum card sharp Gary Gilmour. Gus had 'blossomed' into a fine healthy big lad . . . and what was good enough for Dougie was going to be good enough for him.

While the rest of the team pulled on gear that hadn't seen daylight for many a year, Rodney Marsh the wicketkeeper and myself were about to be 'wired for sound' with a radio microphone.

Australian captain Greg Chappell had won the toss and asked England to bat on a centre wicket area that had withstood the rigours of heavy traffic in a VFL football match less than 48 hours earlier.

It was the ideal time to experiment with sound technology because of the 22 players, Rodney Marsh, Doug Walters, David Hookes, Tony Greig, Bob Willis and myself, were experienced cricket commentators. We were able to understand the discipline needed for describing the game while actually playing to win.

The idea was first talked about during World Series Cricket in the late 70's but had remained dormant until match organiser Rodney Marsh provided the energy and foresight to make it happen. There were only two sets of equipment available and the decision was made to use only fielding players not batsmen.

Both Rodney and myself had special buttondown pockets on our shirts. The shirts, by the way, were like walking billboards with sponsors' logos patched all over them. Actually, if the game had been played under ACB, rules, each player would have been fined many hundreds of dollars for improper product endorsement!

Into the pocket was slipped a battery-operated capsule about the size of a cigarette box. They had a volume control on it and a cord, which connected to a pigmy-sized dummy. This 'dummy' was pushed hard into my ear hole by the sound tech to enable us to hear the program director. He's the guy who decides exactly which one of the many pictures from the various camera positions on the ground go to out and for how long.

It is one thing to stand still with a 'pacemaker' the size of a small transistor radio taped into my shirt pocket but another to have to carry a battery pack in my back trouser pocket. Talk about imbalance. How was a bloke going to be running into bowl?

The battery pack was the size of a brandy flask . . . no spirits just a leather pouch and a slim, black aerial dangled from the device like a fuse. Say the wrong words into the tiny microphone and it could cause almost as much damage as a bomb!

The microphone was attached inside my shirt with double-sided gaffa tape . . . great stuff if you've got a hairy chest! The weight of the bulge in my hip pocket meant that the crutch of my faithful old cricket trousers was constantly around my kneecaps. With an unbecoming, low slung crutch, it was very difficult to get any sort of rhythm in my run up! I felt like a 100 year old with a new pace maker who was tottering around in a baggy pair of 'long-johns', trying to get his hearing aid to work. What'd ya say? What . . .?"

Anyway, we finally got it all to work, although the keeper had a few problems tuning his volume control to the correct position. A case of fingers too large!

Before the match we found ourselves hat in hand looking for worms in the area around deep mid while the national anthem was played . . . No worms on the surface of the hallowed turf and a lot of bloody static in my left ear. Hearing 'God Save our gracious Queen . . .' I got a sniff, so too did the rest of us old timers. Then my heart started pounding, I couldn't help myself, the latent competitive spirit had surfaced. Adrenalin began to flow quickly and freely through my body . . . so too did the thoughts: 'You can beat an egg but you can't beat fixing up a Pom properly! Let's get Pomdinkum and sort this mob out. We can do it!'

I could sense the 39-year-old Dennis Lillee had similar thoughts on his mind, he couldn't wait to scorch Derek Randall's forehead with a bouncer or two and I was hoping the great fast bowler was up to it! He didn't let anyone dwell on the possibility for too long, complete with beard and in the middle of a much publicised comeback, he let a couple go in the first over.

England skipper Tony Greig was occupying the central commentary position and began asking questions of Rod Marsh and myself. 'Bacchus' responding to one such loaded gun, "Considering the night Dennis had, he's bowling pretty well". Already the public were gaining an insight to their heros as never before!

As usual MHN Walker bowled up the hill and into the nasty breeze known affectionately as the Fremantle Doctor. After only two balls the expert comments began from my Nine Network co-commentator and former Test medium pacer, Mick Malone. It was quite off-putting to hear their remarks as I put one foot in front of the other.

Gee, I thought cricket is an easy game from the commentary position and it's very difficult when you haven't played for almost seven years. It would be fair to say that my bowling wasn't exactly showing mid-January form. Every pace I took caused the metal clip supporting the chord to my earpiece to hit me on the skull. It amplified inside my head, like the sound of run away ball bearings.

After a couple of overs of chat, in between balls, my heart rate had definitely increased and so too did my puffing and blowing. This amused both men at the microphones in the rear of the grandstand.

Dogmatic opener Bob Woolmer finally succeeded in smashing me through the covers for a boundary after several misses. From my earpiece came: "What's it feel like to get whacked for four Tangles?"

It was difficult to honestly answer on national television, I was still trying to find a good length. My gut reaction was let's see if he's good enough to do it again. He wasn't. What resulted was a very enthusiastic, "Howzzzaaat?"

Caught Marsh bowled Walker. Just like old times! Brimming with confidence I suggested to Greigy that he ought to slip back to the dressing rooms because it wouldn't be long before I'd be bowling at him.

The friendly banter continued, on cue and with no four letter words or bad manners. What else could one expect in the gentleman's game of cricket! It was great sportsman-like stuff . . . until I asked supposedly the most enlightened cricket brain in the country — Rodney Marsh — a simple question, "Where should I bowl the next one mate?"

The batsman on strike was tailender, John Lever. There were only a few balls remaining of the 49th over. I'm sure you've got your own ideas and so had I . . . and my chunky little mate in pads had his: "A fullish length around leg stump and don't give him any room!"

Should be pretty easy — a yorker around leg stump. But at the back of my mind a little voice kept telling me not to bowl a half volley pitched on middle and leg stump. I should have listened and heeded the advice! No such luck, in the name of good television pictures and commentary, having asked the question and received an answer for everyone to share, there was only one ball to deliver — full on leg stump.

Needless to say the ball bounced once before banging into an advertising sign at deep long on. I got a sunburned roof of the mouth watching it disappear over my right shoulder. "That's the first and last time I'll ever take notice of you . . . !"

England took the field with their two tallest men wired up . . . Bob Willis, the angular fast bowler and Tony Greig. No worries about radio microphone reception with these two mobile aerials!

Greigy enjoyed his role as the verbal villain and loved it when David Hookes — who had smacked him for five consecutive fours in the 1977 classic — was stranded while trying to lift him into the John Inverarity stand.

The big blond off spinner had refused to come face to face with the elegant stroke play of the left-handed Hookes until he was accused of being too frightened to bowl at him. When he did enter the fray, Hookesy peeled 10 off his first over. "Well I can't take myself off now or you will think I'm gutless . . ."

After getting Hookesy, he nominated how he would dismiss the big hitting local Rodney Marsh. "I just keep on tossing 'em up around off stump . . . he won't be able to help himself. He'll hole out in the deep!"

After one bludgeoned boundary that's exactly what happened and our country's former keeper returned to whence he came — the solitude of the dressing room.

Australia won the game in the final over, a very popular result in Perth. After the game the English players even seemed like half reasonable blokes. And to the many thousands of television viewers across the nation, the experiment instigated and carried through by Rodney William Marsh and STW Channel 9 in Perth, was a satisfying first.

There was much reminiscing in the dressing rooms that night long after the floodlights had been switched off, but there was also some discussion on the use of microphones on players both during this game and in the future. Those involved were the four battery carrying crusaders.

Not far away Dennis Lillee couldn't help but overhear the comments . . . and interjected. "You blokes bloody well amaze me. For more than a decade you won't let a television camera near the dressing room, you gave most of the press a wide berth and here you are talking about wiring up players for better tele! You can't mean it! What about the game? Forget about the tele . . . !"

Several beers later he was even more outspoken. Of course Dennis was then contemplating a season in English country cricket in his comeback year, while Rodney, Tony, Bob and myself thought more about how we could better televise cricket.

The Reign of Terror begins

'THAT WAS AFTER HE HAD DRAWN THE CROSS ON HIS FOREHEAD WITH HIS FINGER'

A lot has been written about the so called 'bouncer war' that was supposed to have taken place during the 1974-75 series between England and Australia in the land Down Under.

What is not generally realised is that the opening bullets were fired by Peter Lever and Bob Willis, the two English pace bowlers and to a lesser extent Tony Greig. But in all fairness I must state that it was started by the Englishmen only because we batted first.

The First Test of the series was played on Brisbane's famous Gabba. And before the match was completed it was obvious that one of the greatest fast bowling combinations ever to play Test cricket had been born.

Yes, 'Lillian Thomson' was not an Aussie bird in the outer but two of the fastest bowlers in the world.

It was generally accepted that the Brisbane wicket was, to put it mildly, a trifle unprepared. Torrential Brisbane rain fell on the night before the first day and the honorary curator, who was also the city's Lord Mayor, was forced to abandon the intended Test strip, which had turned into a mud heap, in favor of a wicket a few metres away. Mike Denness remarked that he had never seen a Test wicket quite like it.

Ian Chappell won the toss and chose to bat. Denness must have been delighted not to have to make the decision.

Chappelli, whose *penchant* for the hook shot had lulled the English into a false sense of security, made a fighting 90, but not before he infuriated Tony Greig.

Evidently Tony was a little unhappy about the block mark which had been made on the spot that happened to coincide with the bowler's delivery stride. Exercising his territorial rights over the bowler's crease, Tony scuffed the block hole with his spikes, obliterating it.

Ian Chappell said what followed wasn't a deliberate effort to antagonise Tony Greig; but it certainly had that effect. No sooner was Tony satisfied that he had a more even footing, than Chappell restored his block mark, which Tony once more flattened. This went on for almost five minutes and it required a quiet word in Tony's ear from skipper Denness before the impasse was resolved. Relations between the two players didn't improve when shortly afterwards, Ian Chappell hooked Tony over the fine-leg fence for six.

It wasn't really Tony's day. The incident of the popping crease aside, there were several other words said during the afternoon and to add insult to injury, he was twice warned for running on the pitch. Perhaps it was poetic justice that he finally caught Ian Chappell when he misjudged a hook off Bob Willis.

43

Nor did Tony survive the balance of Australia's first innings without coming in for more critical comment, in particular from Dennis Lillee.

Dennis fell when he had reached 15, and the partnership had added 28 in a manner which caused the words to Tony Greig.

Tony, who had replaced Hendrick at the northern end, decided that as he wasn't having much success in his efforts to beat Dennis' bat, he'd try something different. Accordingly he gave Dennis a bit of a workout, and the second or third bouncer had the desired effect. In attempting to hook the ball, more as a reflex action than a deliberate stroke, Dennis was floored. As he fell, the ball brushed his gloves and he was caught behind by Alan Knott.

It wasn't a pretty sight — the great fast bowler's arms and legs pointing in a heavenly direction — his pride dented beyond belief. And to be given out made it even worse!

At the other end of the wicket stood Tony Greig, legs wide astride like a clothes peg, pointing to the pavilion . . . directing the traffic as always.

The glint and sparkle of success in his eyes gave way to a sarcastic, cutting smile . . . that's why Australians loved to hate him! I knew Dennis was upset when he threw the bat on the ground and it bounced back 18 inches!

He had never seen a Test wicket quite like it.

There is no doubt that the old unwritten rule that fast bowlers do not bowl bouncers at other fast bowlers is now more honored in the breach than in the observance: but that doesn't alter the fact that a fast bowler who receives such treatment is generally somewhat upset when it occurs.

Dennis picked up the bat (upside down) and marched up the pitch. As he drew near the tall former South African, he said, "You'll get yours, sunshine!" and pointed the bat handle straight at Greigy's stomach.

Just to show there were no 'hard feelings', when Tony came in to bat after tea on the second day, he was immediately greeted by a couple of balls from Dennis that nearly took his head off. Perhaps he was lucky that the brunt of the Lillee attack was borne by John Edrich.

By the time their first innings had concluded, the English were starting to realise that the Lillee-Thomson combination was going to give them a great deal of trouble and I think that the ultimate disintegration of their morale began on that second day.

Ian Chappell had an uncanny judgment in assessing a wicket. His ability as a tactician was equally impressive. Normally, he said very little to the players, just left it to the specialists to play their own game in their own way.

His only comment, before we opened our second innings, was a mild request to watch the hook shots — understandable as they had accounted for five of our six wickets in the first innings.

When play resumed on the fourth day we were 95 runs ahead, with Wally Edwards and Ian Chappell both in the pavilion having being dismissed the previous day.

By lunchtime we had added 74 runs for the loss of Redpath, and at the end of the second session, we were 5 for 211 and led by 255.

At this stage, with the temperature hovering around the 35C mark, aggravated by a strong north-westerly that felt as though it was blowing straight from the furnaces of Hades, the attack began to flag allowing Doug Walters and Rod Marsh to hit their way to 77 in 75 minutes.

With 35 minutes remaining to stumps, Ian Chappell declared and Mike Denness was faced with the formidable task of scoring 333 runs in even time to win with a side that had been robbed of its edge by a torrid day in the field. Their position was made even worse because John Edrich's hand was so badly bruised that he could only hold a bat with extreme difficulty.

Had the tourists not been faced with the combination of Lillee and Thomson bowling at their most formidable pace, they may have been able to hang around: but the relief of a draw eluded them and they failed by an hour and 20 minutes and 166 runs. The record books reveal that Jeff Thomson took 6 for 46 in the second innings to give him nine wickets for the match.

But as long as I live, I'll never forget the look on Tony Greig's face when he took block for the first time in the match — he looked back beyond the umpire and there was Lillee half way up the lattice-work on the sight screen, smoke coming out of his ears! I think he was screaming, "I'll get you, you so and so . . ." and that was after he'd drawn the cross on his forehead with his finger. Of course in those days there were no crash helmets!

Greigy had a look around the ground to check out the field placings, two gullies, five slips, Rodney Marsh the keeper, a leg slip and a bat pad and not a soul in front of the wicket anywhere, except for Lillee himself.

I remember Lillee pushing off the sight screen at a million miles an hour and Ian Chappell saying to his mate Marshie, "Is that right? Thommo's taking out Greigy's missus tomorrow night!"

I'll give the big blond his due — he didn' t flinch an eyelid.

Lillee at this stage was poetry in motion — one of the great sights on a cricket ground, providing you hadn't got the bat in your hands.

You don't need to guess where the ball went — it slid past Tony Greig's throat, over Marsh's outstretched hands and into the sight screen for four byes. From then on it was war!

It's history now, that we won again in Perth, Thommo got another seven scalps and by the 4th Test in Sydney we'd won the Ashes . . . a truly unforgettable experience!

Blood on the Wicket
'HIS FACE WAS SWOLLEN UP LIKE A FOOTBALL'

Good old-fashioned blood, guts and determination are three basic ingredients that the average Australian sports fan can immediately relate to during a day at the 'big match' or an evening spent in front of the silver screen.

I guess there is a certain safety in the comfort of your loungeroom, feet up and overflowing Esky at your side, or even in the company of half a dozen bare-chested mates under a blazing sun at the Sydney Cricket Ground.

But for those of us who are given the responsibility of representing our country, state or club at a chosen sport, there is no such safety. For the moment you walk through the gate onto the playing arena you are on your own. Easy game for overheated spectators, biased pressmen or anyone else who cares to take a 'shot' at you.

Generally there is a feeling of apprehension, fear of failure and the heavy burden of a rapidly pounding heart as blood surges through the tightening arteries to the extremities of your body. Adrenalin is released in great quantities as the contest begins — there can be no turning back now.

One of the gutsiest performances I've ever seen on the sporting field occurred during the Centenary Test Match between England and Australia at the MCG in March, 1977. The game itself produced one of the greatest encounters in the history of Test matches played between the two historical arch rivals.

The atmosphere of the crowd during the game was magnificent. It didn't just last for an hour or a session or even a day, it stayed on for five days. As a sportsman I felt very privileged to have played in front of such a wonderfully appreciative crowd.

Rick McCosker will never forget the incident in Australia's first innings. A short-pitched delivery struck the right-handed opening batsman on the side of the face while attempting a hook shot. Rick's jaw was broken in three parts and to add to the agony, the ball dislodged the bails as it fell to the ground. McCosker was out — bowled!

There was an unpalatable silence around the ground as medical men rushed to his aid. Blood quickly turned the batting gloves clenching his face a bright crimson.

The Englishmen were obviously concerned as they encircled the crumpled figure of McCosker. His bat was still resting at the base of the broken stumps as he was helped from the hallowed turf of the MCG.

I first saw the injured batsman as doctors stretched him out on a table in the dim Australian dressing room. There was too much blood for me to handle, one glimpse was enough. Half his face was swollen like a football. It was really quite a sickening and gut-wrenching sight to see one of my team-mates badly injured like that.

Anxiety would be a fair way to describe the feeling with the Australian camp as McCosker was taken to hospital for exhaustive tests and X-rays. The X-rays revealed three fractures on the left side, and his damaged jaw had to be wired. That wiring was to stay in place for more than three weeks.

On the lighter side Rick is a very quiet guy at the best of times but this was ridiculous. Now all we could get out of him was a nod or a shake of the head with maybe a deep grunt in approval.

Doctors warned him not to take any further part in the game. This was like a red rag to a bull. McCosker was a player no matter what, he couldn't get back to his team-mates soon enough. Such was the vast pride the man felt in representing his country at cricket.

It is history now that Rick McCosker did bat for Australia in the second innings but down the batting order instead of his normal opening position.

As Rick walked through the green dressing room door with incredible determination and purpose typical of the guy, 65,000 people stood up and applauded. Our players in the dressing room area pulled back the sliding glass windows to hear the roar. I have never heard that sort of noise from 65,000 Australians. They stood to applaud as he walked down the path towards the white picket fence.

He was bandaged heavily under his chin, over his jaw and around his forehead. He looked like a character from a slapstick movie.

The hair on the back of my neck stood up and I think most people at the ground would have experienced the same sort of sensation. It was indeed a very moving moment.

On his head Rick had the baggy green Australian cap. I'm sure that was the only thing holding McCosker together that day. He was going to represent his country no matter what.

The crowd cheered and began singing, "Waltzing McCosker, Waltzing McCosker . . .", as he positively strode to the wicket tapping the face of his cricket bat into the palm of his left hand, a nervous habit used to relieve the tension.

Can you imagine how he must have felt during that emotional walk to the wicket to do battle with the Englishmen once again! How difficult it must have been to suppress all the negative thoughts of being hit in the face by a cricket ball a day or two earlier.

He took guard on 'middle and leg' as usual and cast an eye around the ground at the opposition field placings. The big crowd cheered as he crouched down over his bat. Anti-hero and England captain, Tony Greig, urged his fast bowler, John Lever, not to relax. McCosker's grim determination to be part of another Australian victory was evident as he hooked the fifth delivery he received behind square leg for four. The 'outer' was ecstatic as the chanting continued.

Rick didn't score a great deal of runs but together with Rodney Marsh (110 not out) the pair added some 30-odd runs. When the final result is considered, I think Rick McCosker's contribution to our win was enormous.

The courageous batsman from NSW received a tumultuous ovation as he left the scene. I just happened to be the next man in and, as I passed Rick at the white gates, I knew it was going to be a difficult act to follow. I'd been dropped down the batting order an extra place, which also put more pressure on me.

When Lillee took the final wicket late on the fifth day of the Test match, Australia had managed to score a memorable victory against England by just 45 runs. Exactly the very same margin of runs as in the first encounter between the two countries 100 years before.

Sitting in the dressing room after play had been completed, with a beer in one hand and a cigarette in the other, Doug Walters made one of the most profound statements of contemporary cricket. With a puff of smoke and a cheeky twinkle in his eye he said, "Well fellas in 100 years of Test Cricket the Poms haven't improved one bloody run, eh?" How true!

Just minutes earlier Dennis Lillee had been chaired shoulder high from the oval after taking six wickets in the first innings and five in the second. It was not to be, but this match could so easily have been Dennis Lillee's last official Test match for Australia. Remember he didn't tour England in 1977, because of a recurring back injury. Three stress fractures of the lower vertebrae were the original problem way back in 1973. Also he had signed to play cricket in Kerry Packer's World Series Cricket during 1977-78.

It must have been tough for McCosker to do anything but grit his teeth, during his stay, because his jaw was wired in three places.

Rick was to be my room-mate on the 1977 tour of England that followed, but because of his jaw being wired, he wasn't able to travel until three weeks after the team arrived in England. Consequently, I had a room to myself which was nice and quiet for a while.

When Rick arrived, back in one piece, I thought, 'This'll be great; someone to talk to'. No such luck. I thought my 'roomie' had forgotten how to talk! After a couple of nights I had to say to him, "Mate, all this noise is killing me. I can't concentrate on my game, I can't go to sleep . . . . you're gonna have to stop asking me all these silly questions!" It didn't take him long before he was chewing the cud and back to normal, telling tall stories and making runs.

When you consider Australia only won the Centenary Test match by 45 runs, Rick McCosker's performance was a match winning innings of vast magnitude.

For the record I did get a hit. I scored 8 of an unbroken 10 run partnership with 'Bacchus' Marsh before my captain Greg Chappell declared at 9/419. I still don't know whether Marshie was embarrassed because I was outscoring him 4-1 or he was just plain tired after his century. But I do know that it was another 50 nipped in the bud, as so often happened during my career with the bat. It was either a case of running out of partners or running out of time.

I can still see Rick McCosker in the dressing rooms. He was sitting on a bench amongst the sweaty ol' shirts and smiling through his clenched teeth at the rest of us singing our victory song:

"Under the Southern Cross I stand

A Sprig of wattle in my hand

A native of this native land

Australia you . . . ."

Thanks mate, you always played the game the way it ought to be played — competitive to the back teeth, but more importantly, like a gentleman.

Perils of a Nightwatchman

'HE'S NEVER SMILED AT AN AUSTRALIAN BATSMAN IN HIS LIFE'

It was well after dark at one of Melbourne's largest football grounds, VFL Park. The digital clock at one end of the ground suggested it was 8.35 p.m. No-one occupied the electronic scoreboard on which the clock was mounted and the huge concrete grandstands were empty, cold and uninviting.

But there was some activity. The cluster of lights hanging in the sky focused like laser beams on 12 of Australia's finest criketers. They were huddled around a plain old cardboard carton, intent on taking the gentleman's game into a whole new dimension.

Inside the much used carton were between 20 to 30 cricket balls. Every colour in the rainbow seemed to be represented — there were yellow ones, white ones, pink ones, pale blue, orange, even a bright red one!

Yes, This was how night cricket began, as an experiment with coloured balls under lights at VFL Park. I must admit I arrived at the ground that night thinking it was just a crazy idea. How could any batsman be expected to see 5½oz of leather hurtling down the wicket towards him in the middle of the night and consistently hit it. Well, by the end of the night it was obvious the cricket could be played at night and Kerry Packer immediately spent millions of dollars on it. The cardboard box and coloured balls was the 'cheap' feasibility study, what followed was the monolithic light pylons at the Sydney Cricket Ground.

White balls were selected and coloured clothing quickly followed, mainly because of the umpiring difficulties in 'seeing' the white ball against white pads.

Australia was lemon, which really set off the road maps in the eyeballs after a night out on the town. Wicketkeeper, Rodney Marsh, the man with billiard table legs, was the Aussie model. The West Indies were given a colour which very much resembled 'nipple pink'. Can you imagine the world's No.1 batsman Viv Richards in nipple pink? It was a sight, particularly if he batted all night, which he often did. The other problem with the 'Windies' colour was that pink in the Caribbean was the gay colour and I couldn't blame 'em for grizzling. And giant South African born Tony Greig looked like an oversize plastic clothes peg, the first time he strutted his stuff in the pale blue of the World X1 colours.

The introduction of night cricket changed many aspects of the game. It had a dramatic affect on me, especially as a batsman. You can't overlook talent forever and the good judges of a batsman in my time — like captains Ian and Greg Chappell — didn't. They looked very seriously at the talent batting ability of Maxwell Henry Norman Walker for the role of night watchman and I didn't let them down! Well I didn't in the daytime.

Now the 'nightwatchman' is usually a batsman not good enough to bat regularly. Against his will or better judgement he has to go to the wicket for a few minutes before stumps to protect the so called 'good batsmen' for another day! Usually these better players are settled back in the dressing room; boots and socks off, feet up on the window sill, reading the paper.

Whereas the poor old 'nightwatchy' is usually poised on the edge of his chair, buttock muscles cramped and trying not to stain his jock strap. At the same time he is attempting the impossible — biting his nails through the heavy padding of the batting gloves. He has one eye on the cricket — playing each ball from the sideline, heart pounding against his ribcage — while the other eye watches just how slowly the second hand can move around the clock face.

When I look back on my evenings as a nightwatchman I guess I was pretty lucky. In Test matches I never did get to make that agonisingly long, lonely and slow walk, to the centre wicket area as 11 sets of beady eyes bored in to add to the pressure. But during the two pioneering years of World Series Cricket, a lot of things changed under the tee-shirt slogans of 'Big Boys Play at Night' and 'Come see the White Ball Fly', including the role of the nightwatchman. For no longer did he have to go in at 10 minutes to six. Try something like 10.20 p.m. at night!

The great players did it and that made an average player look more confident. You would have a bit of a look around the ground, from third man, through mid off, way down to long leg. You just may bluff the opposition 'quick' into thinking that you can play shots all around the wicket — and we all know that the worst thing a fast bowler can do is think, don't we? Not too many of 'em are Rhodes Scholars and I mean that in the nicest possible way because some of my best mates are former fast bowlers! The moment of truth is getting nearer. Sooner or later you will have to more than just look good. A batsman is only allowed to fiddle with his boot laces and tighten the top buckle of both pads for a few moments, otherwise it will look like you're stalling for time and an umpire doesn't have to be Albert Einstein to come to that conclusion.

Ready. Place one foot either side of the batting crease and start tapping the bat on the ground in anticipation while holding the handle with the grip of a wood chopper. You're looking like one of those black & white 'pitchers' in Sir Donald Bradman's coaching manual — chin tucked into the shoulder and eyes looking up towards the umpire. Even though the visor of the crash helmet is fogged up through being hot under the collar and the adrenalin is starting to flow freely through the body, try and manage a smile at the umpire, because he may just keep his hands in his pockets a little longer, especially if it's a cold night. Maybe he is recalling what Confucious say, "Little boy with one hole in pocket feel cocky all day" and "Little boy with two holes in pockets leaves no stone unturned!" Anyway, all the men in white used to be little boys at some stage of their life and dare I say it, many still are!

Then look back beyond the umpire and there he is — Joel Garner, — the giant calypso quick, standing in front of a black sight screen. 'Big Bird' is not half past eleven, he's midnight. Very dark. He's never smiled at an Australian batsman in his life and isn't about to now. Even if he did all you would see would be something like a massive piano key board!

Garner and three or four of his long-legged team-mates all have the ability to bowl at about 150-160 kmh. This means you've got about 0.25 seconds to play forward, back or simply duck and get out of the way! How are you feeling now? Decidedly sick and scared I bet!

Brace yourself as the 'Bird' pushes off the sight screen. Honestly, all you can see at first is a white cricket ball suspended in space about a metre above a white shirt. As he changes towards the umpire, set against the black background, his bulging eyes look like ping pong balls. The pounding of his massive feet sounds like a herd of elephants. Still a few paces to go then he gets up high on his toe-nails in the final delivery stride . . . an awful sight!

Just as his huge bunch of fives is about to launch that leather missile, imagine that one of those fat moths that buzz around the lights at the SCG flutters into the slot between the helmet visor and your perspiring face. What do you do? You can't extend your hand down the wicket like a traffic cop to stop all oncoming traffic! You can't shout at the top of your voice, "Hang on Joel . . . till I get rid of this dirty big moth!" There is no way he will hear over the roar of 40,000 fans. You can't put a hand up the visor because your fingers and thumb are double the thickness in gloves. They won't fit!

There is only one answer — open your mouth as wide as you possibly can! The moth's legs wedge in your throat and the clapping wings soon stick like glue to the saliva on the roof of your mouth.

While this activity is taking place inside your mouth, Joel Garner has let one go, straight at the target. You know very well that the ball is going to crash into your rib-cage with a sickening thud. It's pitched about half way down the wicket and climbing rapidly and those lines of stitching are steering the sphere at you. Bullseye!

It's often been said that pain is only one deep and I couldn't agree more! Ask the bloke down at the non-strikers end, who is smugly leaning on his brand new bat, if he knows what it feels like to have a couple of ribs broken by a cricket ball. Most probably he explains in an understanding manner that he knows exactly how much it hurts. But you know bloody well he's lying — the alarm bells are ringing inside your ribs not his.

With that kind of experience behind you, I'm sure that you'll agree that watching a 'nightwatchman' trying to get his act together against a great 'faster', who has just come back into the attack to take the new ball, is a very entertaining exercise for everyone except the poor old nightwatchman.

It's been a few years since I was last called in as a nightwatchman. But those other good judges of talent — the Tattslotto management in Melbourne — looked closely at me and put me in to 'bat' at 5.58 p.m., six nights a week, on TV.

This was for the new gambling game of Keno. With my experience around that time of night, I guess I was going to be a natural. Playing Keno and being a 'nightwatchie' is very similar and both are played with coloured balls. In cricket, it's a matter of spotting the shiny red or white ball (depending on when you play) and matching your batting skills. If you're lucky and play the correct shot, you're still in the game and you get another chance. Not so different really to spotting a series of numbers at Keno and matching them. If you're skilful, or should I say lucky, you're a winner in this game with the sporting elements of spot, match, win.

Nowadays when I walk to the 'wicket' as a nightwatchman it is usually with a fair application of make-up and some-eye-drops to make my murky green eyes sparkle under the lights. I'm also dressed in a swish dickie bird suit and a snappy little bow-tie.

The floor manager counts down — 5, 4, 3, 2, 1 — then he signals 'play' like an umpire with a drop of the hand. A red light on top of camera No. 2 flashes like an ambulance and an audience of three government officials sit, stern-faced in judgement, at 'square leg'. These days I'm confident, so bring on those coloured balls . . .

As if I never stopped

'I DEFINITELY HAD A SNIFF NOW. THE COMPETITIVE URGE WAS UNDOUBTEDLY THERE'

Australia is very fortunate to have such a sports fanatic as Bob Hawke as our Prime Minister. Mr. Hawke loves all sports but his first love is cricket . . . not that he gets to play much of the gentleman's game these days, maybe one or two matches each year.

It was my privilege to have the Prime Minister as my captain in the traditional Politicians v Crusaders contest at the Melbourne Cricket Ground in February, 1986.

The tranquility of standing at deep-mid off on the hallowed MCG turf and looking around the empty grey stands that enclose the famous old cricket ground was just about as far as Mr Hawke could get from politics . . . and he was out to make the most of the day.

Not one to shirk his responsibilities though, a special phone hook-up had been arranged by his office, just in case he needed to leave the field in a hurry.

The politicians were in the field first against a pretty strong looking Crusaders line-up. Ian Chappell, in a very rare appearance, had been recruited by the Crusaders' founder and human dynamo, Swan Richards, of Gray-Nicolls cricket bat fame.

Swan said of Chappelli, "He's possibly the greatest captain the game's ever seen and he bats a bit, so if he can't get us up then nobody can!"

Well the Prime Minister and his colleagues had news for Swan Richards and his lads in this, the fifth encounter between the two teams. They play for the Burley Griffin trophy — an intricate sculpture by a jewellery designer named John Atherton. John is the guy who hand-tooled the first gold cricket bat to hang around the vigorous neck of the world's greatest fast bowler — Dennis Lillee!

When Bob Hawke gave me the new ball from the members end, it felt momentarily like old times. Just a blink of the eyes and images of 65,000 screaming fans came flooding back as we bowled England out for 95 on the second day of the Centenary Test match in March, 1977.

My heart started to pound a bit and the butterflies inside my stomach began to assemble in a straight line . . . a couple of agonising stretches, attempting to touch my toes, brought too much blood to my head . . . I came up for air!

The comforting feeling of a brand new Kookaburra cricket ball in my hand was all I needed — I definitely had a sniff now. The competitive urge was undoubtedly there!

As I pushed off from the head of my bowling mark it was almost as if I'd never stopped playing . . . except for the mature waistline.

Dr John Lill, the former South Australian batsman and secretary of the prestigious Melbourne Cricket Club, opened the batting as if it was a Test match . . . he complained quietly about the bare black patch of compressed mud which had a few grass shavings thrown in for good measure.

But as my other opening bowler, South Australian captain and former Test batsman, David Hookes, pointed out to him — "Don't blame the . . . wicket, you made it. If you're not happy — fix it!"

Maybe that innings of 53 (retired) by the former champion batsman gave him a better insight into the centre-wicket controversy that had hounded his curator Jack Lyons. Still, it was a knock sprinkled with a touch of class and he strode off the big arena a happy man.

But the focus was now clearly on the form of legendary captain Ian Chappell after an absence of five years.

Little had changed from the 'golden days' — the tug of the cap, the grope at his abdominal protector and the shuffle of the rubber-soled shoes!

He always valued the price of his wicket very highly and I could tell today was going to be no casual, social outing for Chappell.

It was a huge relief for him when the first one hit the bat. Quickly his footwork began to fall into place against the spinners. His teeth clenched tightly when I was brought back into the attack.

The colourful right hander hit several spanking cover drives to thrill the crowd of about 300 journalists and friends.

The scoreboard showed 51 (retired) against the famous name as he made his compulsory departure . . . maybe for the last time. Probably never again will we witness Ian Chappell score a half-century at the MCG.

Somehow the Crusaders scrambled to a respectable 7-192 from their allotted 40 overs. and it should be noted that the quite formidable batting skills of Sir Billy Snedden weren't called upon — he was listed at No. 11.

Victorian Cricket Association Secretary, Ken Jacobs, became the PM's only wicket for the day. The scorebook said: "K. Jacobs — st Dimattina b Hawke, 7."

Mr. Hawke reflected on the delivery. "It bounced a lot, after gripping the wicket and turning viciously past the outside face of the bat." Some wise cracker in the field — and I'm sure it came from an Opposition member — said, "Just as well you were successful that time, Dimattina or you would have been banished to South Africa!"

I must admit I was pleased to take my boots off after 10 overs or should I say 60 balls . . . gee the old feet were really barking! I guess they hurt even more seeing I failed to take a wicket. A good player out of luck, couple of easy catches dropped.

Our hopes were pinned on two Test batsmen, Ross Edwards and David Hookes, getting most of the runs, but that was not to be!

Edwards (11) was sensationally caught and bowled in the fourth over of the innings by Swan Richards — just a few weeks late for the Classic Catches competition on Channel 9. Bill Lawry would have loved it. 'Swannie' hasn't stopped talking about it.

Hooksey hit three fours and two sixes in a whirlwind 26.

But really it was left to Mr Hawke batting at No. 4 and MHN Walker batting well below ability at No. 10.

The PM wasn't hooking at all after his 1985 experience but was in fine touch with his drives . . . if only he hadn't pursued politics, he may have played for his country.

It was like turning the clock back 30 years, when 'Typhoon' Tyson, bowling fractionally slower, charged in from the members end. Frank Tyson crippled the Australian batting line-up here in 1955, taking seven very cheap wickets in a devastating display of fast bowling. Today Frank lives in Australia and is Director of Coaching with the VCA.

Bob Hawke (31) was caught out by journalist Ken Piesse, from the cunning spin of retired politician, Tony Street, who returned the exceptional figures of 4-15.

So at 8-120, chasing 192, we were in big trouble.

I was quick to sum up the situation — we weren't going to win it by blocking, which suited my game fine. Some rear-guard pinch-hitting was required.

And with one over to go — 13 runs were needed. Swan Richards was asked to bowl with yours truly on strike — not an easy task.

Two, two, two, four and three resulted in a win for us with a ball to spare — Swannie was devastated.

The Prime Minister was ecstatic — he'd guided another team to victory and he won the 'Man of the Match' as well.

Chapter Three

A GRIN A DAY IN THE EARLY YEARS

He'd waddled out to the packed main bar.

A Pain in the Rear End
'MAYBE HE JUST LIKED OUR DUNNY'

Living in a pub during my early adolescent years brought me face-to-face with some great characters.

One of the more colourful identities who would regularly pay us a visit was a large tram conductor — I'm not sure of his name! Not that I ever spoke to him — all I did was stare!

Just like clockwork, almost to the minute every day, at about 10.15 a.m., this giant of a man, dressed in his plain, navy blue tramways uniform, would sneak in through the Burnett Street entrance to the pub — hoping nobody would see him as he raced down the corridor to the gents' toilet and relief!

His constitution must have been like clockwork too — at the same time, at the same place, every day of the working week! Or maybe he just liked our 'dunny' — we'll never know!

He used to time his run beautifully, despite not being blessed with much natural pace. Off he'd run as soon as the driver had stopped the tram! The driver then clocked on at the green tramway key clock, fixed to an ageing telegraph post not far from the traffic lights at Elizabeth and Burnett Streets. It was just across from the red brick building known to all affectionately as The Empire! A good beer drinking hotel.

This stopover used to generally last between two or three red light changes . . . it also gave his driver a chance to have a quiet smoke!

Looking back, the catastrophic events of one visit were very funny to everyone present at the watering hole at the time except for our over-weight, lead-footed clippy!

It wasn't number ones he wanted to do, it definitely was number twos — some belly ache, eh? All 20 stone of him rumbling . . . the mind boggles! Probably two or three pies inside that stomach without even teethmarks on them. He was a big boy!

Well, it just so happened that our desperate hulk of a man was a bit like the late Howard Hughes — a cleanliness freak! Worried about catching something off the toilet set and all that silly rot.

It was a silly consideration anyway because our sparkling white porcelain bowls didn't have a timber seat — plastic wasn't invented then! There were too many vandals around and the odd, eccentric drinker who thought they'd made a good picture frame — so my dad 'Big Max' cut his costs and left his clientele to put up with an occasional cold bottom during the winter months.

Seeing this, our regular Trammie somehow climbed successfully on top of the bowl to avoid contamination and quickly took up a 'kangaroo' style squat.

The fragile porcelain fixture was supporting his entire body weight because now both feet were on either side of the pan. But that's not the end of the story.

Unfortunately for him that day, the porcelain bowl shattered during proceedings with disastrous effects . . . I heard the poor man's frightened scream in the kitchen. By the time I rushed to the WC to see what was happening, he'd courageously waddled out to the packed main bar.

There he stood — his blue trousers crumpled around his thick, hairy ankles. Blood was streaming down his right hamstring from a nasty deep gash in his buttocks — it wasn't a pretty sight, and I was standing behind him! It took a doctor and 23 stitches to stem the flow.

All the time he was standing there, he continually shouted profanities about Big Max and his bloody toilets.

The 'fallen hero' of Hobart's trams was going to sue my dad for having faulty fittings in his toilets and causing grievous bodily harm.

Some months later, the case did go before the courts of Hobart . . . the judge had this to say in his summation of the unfortunate incident, "In my view it was an unnatural technique for a normal action. Had the victim had both feet on the ground at the time of the accident, he may have had a case, but he didn't! Case dismissed!"

I suppose you can be unlucky.

Funny how that tram never used to stay long at the tramway clock on the corner of Burnett and Elizabeth Streets, North Hobart. After the grief it caused, the conductor must have spent weeks getting over the injury, with his right cheek buried in a tractor inner-tube . . . well, it wouldn't fit in a car-tube, would it?

One of my other favorite characters was a poor nameless soul who lived on sweet sherry. He had a face that had done a million miles, with heavy lines etched deep into his leathery skin. In fact his mouth was like a torn pocket.

Above his bushy eyebrows was a beautifully polished bald head with a horseshoe shaped layer of hair circumnavigating just above his ears. Those large ears were something else too. They looked for all the world like a huge set of amplifiers and not much got past them either!

He had been banned from the premises more often than my old man could remember. Yet, he still continued to drink at the Empire. Always in a stupor, his survival prompted an amusing albeit predictable performance from staff and drinkers. As he was ushered from one bar, he would take to the street, and immediately enter another bar. Five steps forward and three steps back . . . it was a struggle, but he always succeeded in getting to the next bar.

He had been ejected from all three bars with a street entrance, and before my dad could give him a decent boot up the backside, his eyes used to stick out like golf balls.

Amazed, he'd question my father: "How many more bloody hotels in Hobart do ya own Max?"

The Sinking of HMAS Maxie
'I STAYED ON BOARD RIGHT UNTIL THE END'

One day in 1985, Doug Walters and myself were locked away in a recording studio in Melbourne to do some radio commercials for the beer they named after Dougie's batting average in England — Toohey's 2.2! Well, that's what Dougie reckoned — I reckon he's being a bit hard on himself.

During the recording, Doug got around to discussing my ability to wind-surf. Mind you, it's not much better than his.

Dougie asked me where I'd received the huge bump on the head. Even though my tongue-in-cheek topical reply of, "I ran into a Russian freighter off the coast of New Zealand!" was scripted, the more I think about it the possibility of it actually happening seemed very real. Especially after a holiday in Fiji where I tackled the sport for the first time.

It's true about my being unco-ordinated hence the nickname 'Tanglefoot', — and sailboarding is no pursuit if you're not pretty on your feet.

Nevertheless, I entertained the front beach at the Hyatt Regency Hotel for almost an hour without actually getting a ride. As well as the humiliation, I lost several inches of skin off both knee-caps by trying to stay in contact with the abrasive surface on the sailboard.

I doubt very much whether I spent any more than 15 seconds standing upright, with the mast in a vertical position, at any one attempt. In my defence it was a very windy day. But what's the point if there's no wind — a bronzed Aussie like myself would then only become becalmed.

Day two was much more successful . . . me and my machine actually drifted with the current about 45 metres before I fell off! Pretty sharp coral that Fijian stuff! A nasty gash and bruise appeared on the fleshy part of my left buttock. By the end of the week it looked like the rings of Saturn, ranging from purple to green.

On a previous holiday, I had a more successful attempt at another exciting and exhilarating water sport — para-gliding. Gee, it's fantastic.

My little adventure hanging under the colourful silk canopy and being pulled by a speedboat, occurred off the back beach at the fabulous holiday resort of Great Keppel Island.

My problem was landing. If the left-hand harness strap is tugged, then supposedly the parachute will drop away to the left. That's where the beach was and that's where I ended up. Ended up's right! I landed not quite so elegantly as ballet dancer, but accurately, on the water's edge. The speedboat cut its engines as I was the last ride and it was getting too windy. Too windy would be the understatement of the day. As I landed, the force of the wind in the large yellow and black parachute, pulled my hopelessly tangled body effortlessly along the beach.

Everybody thought it a great joke except me. The sand felt like sandpaper on my kneecaps, and the result was the same as the sailboarding — badly skinned knees.

The next day I wanted to go jet-skiing, but no way. I could hardly walk. Every step I took opened the healing skin. A bit like smiling when your lips are cracked and sunburnt. And to jet-ski, it's a kneeling start.

So it's no wonder I'm not a super big wrap for the aquatic pursuits of this world. Maybe it's because my childhood days were spent in Tasmania where the murky green waters that lap the tiny island coastline, are icy-cold even in mid-summer.

I was even unlucky with water in those early years. The sense of adventure in my childhood character was just beginning to surface then — or should I say sink.

It was a bleak winter's day in Hobart. My freckle-faced friend, John, and myself, both aged a mere nine years, were looking for excitement, so we decided that 'sailing' was our go . . . and off we set.

We were very limited in experience at anything nautical, let alone sailing, but we went ahead enthusiastically to 'construct' a raft, and I do use that term 'construct' very loosely! The chance of it not floating never entered my mind. Kids really are very positive thinkers at that age!

Our small raft was made from four old-fashioned, square kerosene drums which were fixed together by some rusty, twisted wire and covered by a flimsy platform of rejected timber planks. It was the sort of stuff every kid dreams of, straight out of the Boys Own Annual!

The venue for our epic voyage was an unloved quarry site, no longer used. At the base of the stark, rocky cliff face was a large waterhole. I had visions of floating out into the middle of the pond, where all the big frogs and 'taddies' might be, so too did my mate John!

As I was three months older, I was the senior partner and of course it meant that I had the final say. So yours truly got to sail our wonderful creation on its maiden voyage . . .

We looked around for a mast and sailcloth but it was definitely 'too hard'. No cloth. And anyway how does a kid fix a buckled piece of 4" x 2" to a few uneven weatherboard planks? Use skyhooks?

A decision was immediately made to reach the distant cliff face by paddling. Unfortunately for me, the further our primitive vessel travelled across unknown waters, the more muddy water my tiny ballast tanks accepted. The platform was soon beginning to tilt badly to one end. The water level too was creeping up the side of each of the cans. All the signals were there!

Just like on that fatal day with the Titanic, the unbelievable happened. Yes, the HMAS Maxie slowly sank.

Being the loyal skipper that I was, I stayed on board, right until the end. Well, there was nowhere else to go and after all, it was July! By this stage I was desperately conscious of just how cold pond water can be, even when fully clothed.

My shout for help raised only a nervous laugh from Johnny who looked pleased to be wearing dry clothing and standing at the edge of the pond.

As for myself, well, only my neck remained visible as I thrashed frantically to stay afloat. Luckily I had just learned to swim. Nevertheless my soggy clothing was very heavy and made swimming most difficult. I didn't panic but fear enveloped my soul as my heart started pounding faster than my arms were flailing. Who said if you open your eyes under water it's possible to view a wonderland? This place wasn't exactly the Barrier Reef. I couldn't see three inches in front of my nose.

Eventually I dragged myself out of the icy water with trousers and shirt clinging to my trembling, goose-pimpled skin. I vowed then and there that I wouldn't grapple with mother nature again.

What could I tell my Mum? A few white lies maybe? They didn't work! And I received the biggest thrashing of my life. I didn't see Johnny for a week or two either.

Pointing in the right direction

'BAZZA MacKENZIE WOULD HAVE BEEN PROUD OF HIM'

I can vaguely remember the night. It was New Year's Eve, 1962. A few months earlier I had celebrated my 14th birthday with a few school mates — the strongest drink in sight that night was Coca Cola. How in the course of just three months things can change, eh?

Being a young man of inquiring mind, and also the son of a hotel proprietor meant that a glass of beer and I weren't exactly strangers. In fact, it was not unusual for my old man to allow me the taste of an odd beer or two. His theory was he might as well give it to me himself rather than hear of his boy acquiring the amber fluid by devious means. And that was fair enough!

But he took his philosophy a step further amidst those New Year's Eve celebrations at our hotel — The Empire Hotel, Elizabeth Street, North Hobart. My dad had decided to deter my liking for the front bar's standard line — a 7 oz with a head please!

His efforts proved to be fairly successful as I recall. After about 16 glasses of beer which I had been unknowingly encouraged to consume, it was my opinion I'd had enough. So had my 13-year-old cousin Michael, who had also unwittingly become a victim!

It had already been a big night for all concerned, especially The Empire Darts Club players who were enjoying the contents of a free keg of

Cascade. Supper consisted of a huge feed of fish and chips from George's Fish Supply. Michael and I had placed the order and delivered the goods, much to the delight of the beer-swilling crowd.

My father, 'Big Max', threatened us with a fate worse than death if we didn't drink another two glasses of beer. A difficult task too, because I could feel the water line inside my body around the gum line on my bottom teeth — and that is full!

No sooner had my younger cousin emptied his final 7 oz glass, than Big Max who, by the way stood about 6'3" and weighed 17 stone at least, picked the little fellow up in both hands, raising him above his head.

It only took about three revolutions, like a helicopter blade cutting the air, for this exercise to take effect. Michael landed at the base of the staircase leading to the house guests' rooms. He took one step, and 'threw' the entire contents of his tummy on to the eighth step of the floral carpeted stair with all his heart and soul. Bazza Mckenzie would have been proud of him!

I really did feel crook. Someone suggested I ought to go to bed — I agreed. The only problem being that the moment my head touched the pillow, the walls started spinning and the ceiling closed in on me! Some smarty said, "Why don't you turn him over? That'll fix him!"

It did, because moments later I too became very ill — and those hotel room hand basins only hold so much, don't they?

My lesson had been learned the hard way — my dad had succeeded.

Four years later, the time following my Matriculation exams, gave me an appropriate excuse to sample the fine water again but I was still to be convinced of its merits!

By January, 1967, my sporting career had taken me to Melbourne to play Australian Rules football with the Melbourne Football Club. This enabled me to pursue my cricket ambitions with the Melbourne Cricket Club as well and to study architecture at the Royal Melbourne Institute of Technology.

In those days I aspired to be a Test batsman but my efforts in my district cricket debut were not sensational. No wicket for 45 runs off five overs was the result in my first match and a duck first ball with the bat.

But when I took five wickets in just my second outing in district cricket it seemed a fair enough reason to 'break out' again. My drinking partner for the night was team-mate, Peter Smith, the son of legendary Melbourne Football Club coach, the late Norman Smith. Norm was the man who would coach me in my first VFL game of football against North Melbourne.

As I was new in Melbourne, Peter Smith invited me to stay over at his place, especially since the game in question was played just up the road from his parents' house at Pascoe Vale.

Peter and I arrived home around midnight in less than a fantastic state. How we drove between the two brick posts into the neat driveway still amazes me.

Now the Smith family was a very close-knit family. Whilst I wobbled from left to right in the coach's bedroom doorway, Pete attempted to kiss his mum goodnight. The result was . . . Peter landed on top of a sleeping Norm on the other side of the bed and caught him a nasty blow to the groin with his knee . . . what a way to be woken up, eh?

At this stage the atmosphere in the house was electric. It really isn't much fun when you're in a strange house with nowhere to go.

Marj, Pete's mum, was really paying out on him, when she turned to me and said, "You boys have been drinking haven't you?" I replied honestly saying, "Yes, just a little." I didn't sleep much that night — maybe I felt guilty?

Daylight arrived all too soon. This time it was Norm who was paying out on Peter — he was in tears as he left the house through the back door.

What does a bloke do when his mate's in trouble — you try to help. So I followed my mate to the door when I heard Norm say, "Pull up a chair son."

I was frozen because I had heard some of those vivid stories of Norm Smith verbally ripping strips of flesh from many of his senior players in the privacy of the property steward's room at the MCG. I too had seen grown men leave that room with wet eyes and emotionally shaken by the words of the red-haired coach.

As I pulled up the chair my eyes focused on the red and white fleck laminex table top. Marj was doing the washing up — you wouldn't reckon a woman doing a small amount of washing up could make so much noise.

The next 20 minutes or so were quite revealing. My future senior coach described my obligations to the Melbourne Football Club, himself, my parents and most of all, myself. At this stage I had not attended any pre-season practice for the MFC — they were to begin in late January.

Then we eye-balled each other for the first time that morning. He set about philosophising about the pros and cons of drinking so clearly, that as I look back on my entire sporting career, both football and cricket, this was the most important moment of my life. It was at this point that I decided not to have another drink.

His parting words on the subject were, "We will not discuss this topic again, you're big enough and ugly enough to make up your own mind."

I knew he meant it too — then he challenged me to a game of tennis. At 50 plus years of age, yes Norm Smith proved too hot for me to handle. Down I went 6-1, 6-1, 6-0 — even at that age the man was a fierce competitor.

Time passed very rapidly during the next couple of years for me as new challenges appeared almost daily. My life's commitment was now to being successful at VFL football, cricket and also as a student of architecture.

Not many challenges were more difficult than the rejection almost daily of the great Aussie invitation "D'ya wanna beer, mate?" There was a continual pressure by my peer group for "Go for it" as they'd say or, "Don't be weak." Believe me it took a lot of strength to say, "No" and mean it.

Things may have changed a lot these days and even towards the end of

my cricket career I may have indulged in just one or two. Ask any of my friends at Bay 13 or fine leg at the MCG or any other ground for that matter.

When I accepted a spectator's drink, I was accepting them and their mates. It would immediately open up a line of communication. There probably is no better way to have a chat than over a drink whether it be in a bar or at the cricket.

I've made some great friends on the other side of the fence. Late in the day, under the hot burning sun, they can come in pretty handy. At some grounds you can almost nominate your drink. BUT a word of warning: make sure YOU pull the top of the can, because boys will be boys and they will get up to some terrible tricks if you let them.

I suppose the moral of the story is, if you want to be successful at anything, you must first assess the cost and just how badly you want to be successful. Unfortunately you can't be one of the boys every night of the week and a talented athlete on weekends — the scales will never balance.

Fortunately for me I ran into Norm Smith at the right time of my life — and I thank him very much for pointing me in the right direction.

Sordid Saga of the Money Box

'SHE LEAPT NAKED FROM THE BED, SWEARING LIKE A WHARFIE'

For a young man barely past the age of puberty, a hotel was hardly the ideal place in which to be brought up. Nevertheless, it did provide me with a wonderful street education.

At the age of 14, I believed I truly was a man of the world after witnessing the arrest of Francey-Ann, a prostitute with flaming red hair, who was known as much for her fits of rage as for the services offered at unexceptional rates.

My adventure began when my sister reported that her money box and beloved Beatles record collection had been stolen. The police promptly were called and officers immediately made a search of the 12 accommodation rooms at the hotel.

They were hardly surprised to find the goods in a room occupied — that is when schedules dictated — by Francey-Ann.

At the time of the police raid, she was in bed with a very drunk Chinese sailor. The lady was very upset by the intrusion and in the most colourful language possible told police officers, hotel staff and yours truly that these accusations were a very serious slur on her impeccable character.

My vantage point through all this was the narrow crack in the door.

Offended by the barrage of laughter her remarks had drawn, she became enraged. Swearing like a wharfie, she leapt naked from the bed and threw her stiletto-heeled shoes at the nearest police officer.

Swearing like a wharfie, she leapt naked from the bed.

As policemen queued for the right to make the necessary rugby tackle, she made for the window.

The police then thwarted her get-away bid and while two burly police officers held her by the ankles to make sure she did not complete a dive from the second storey window, the tiny sailor got dressed in silence and exited quietly.

Francey-Ann was charged with possession of stolen goods, prostitution, resisting arrest and a few other offences, while her amorous client returned to the docks.

For many weeks, I was the toast of the schoolyard as my friends and others gathered to hear my version of how Francey-Ann was apprehended. I might add that with each hearing I used artistic licence and added what might be termed embellishments — for my dad once told me: "Son, never muck up a good story for the facts."

The pub provided for me the opportunity to tell many a story. Not all were as titillating as FA, but nevertheless, it was this early environment which encouraged me to share my experiences — some seamy, but many humorous.

Next door to our hotel was the oil-caked premises of Frank Hammond Pty Ltd Trucking Services. The company carried many consignments of 44-gallon drums, and often had drums both full and empty stored at the bottom of the yard. On one unusually hot day the metal drums expanded, the bungs leaked and tar oozed out under the fence into the fowlyard at the back of the Empire Hotel.

When Elvie the cook went to feed our fowls at about five o'clock, she found some of them stuck, and the tar beginning to set hard. My old man immediately assured Elvie and me that everything was under control and that the situation could be remedied easily.

He strode into the fowlyard and put both hands under one of the fowls and vigorously pulled it from its fixing. Believe me, the technique was crude, but very effective, except that its two feet and 'drumsticks' stayed anchored in the black tar.

Not easily deterred, dad produced a chisel from his tool box and as delicately as possible chipped around the feet of another stunned hen, leaving it with two solid black squares of tar stuck to its claws.

That worked, too, except that it could not fly and kept slipping off the perch. The final result was that this hen and a few of her mates died of fatigue four days later.

A witness to all this was a great pal of mine, Paddy, my pet boxer dog. Unfortunately, I did not have the same control over him as I occasionally had with a cricket ball.

Paddy was well-known to the drinkers at the pub and was the nemesis of postmen, policemen on the beat, women in expensive hose and children intent on stealing our empty soft drink bottles from the bottom of the backyard.

To the acute embarrassment of Big Max, Paddy's name was on file at the Tasmanian Tourist Bureau.

A most incredible happening led to him being regarded as an impediment to local tourism.

As a kid, I enjoyed many hours playing cricket with reprobates, who spent most of their waking hours at the hotel. I would lure them into batting or bowling as they went to and from the gents' lavatory at the back of the building.

One such time, a drunk managed to straight drive me through the open window of one of the accommodation bedrooms. The ball bounced off the window sill, landing on the lap of an unsuspecting guest resting on a bed. Paddy, who was trained to retrieve cricket and tennis balls, scrambled up the metal fire escape stairs on to the roof and from the window ledge leapt on to the guest to recover the ball.

The indignant visitor promptly contacted the tourist bureau, asked for alternative accommodation and implored officers not to send any more guests to the Empire as there was a mad adolescent armed with a cricket ball and a wild dog loose in the grounds.

On one occasion my dad had to call on his carpentry skills due to Paddy's appetite.

The sight of steak being beaten by the kitchen staff so overwhelmed the dog that he crashed through the window, showering glass and pinning Elvie, resplendent in pinafore, to the floor.

In a gesture of apology, he licked the cook's face before chewing the tassels of her well-worn slippers and making off with the meat. Too shrewd, my mate.

The Man in White is Right

'THE PAY OFF WAS TO HAVE BEEN TWO TRUCK LOADS OF POTATOES . . .'

Isn't it amazing how players make mistake after mistake in sporting contests, yet let an umpire make just one bad decision during the course of events, and all hell breaks loose?

In every walk of life there needs to be an arbitrator — someone who has the authority to umpire a dispute.

At the top of our legal system, it's generally an eagle-eyed old man, with a white curly wig on top of his very experienced and learned head, who sits in judgment — he's respected and well-paid.

But in sport, it's usually the opposite. In junior sport the job of umpiring some games is mostly the responsibility of keen, enthusiastic parents who are paid absolutely nothing for their time. It's a labour of love and a chance to watch their kids grow up.

To many spectators of sport, the umpire is the lowest form of life on the playing field, and they constantly remain a great object for releasing the pent-up frustrations of the spectator.

Even international umpires receive 'peanuts' in payments compared to the players who compete under their astute direction.

For example, the majority of people involved in umpiring professional tennis, do so for little more than 'expenses' and believe me, they get very little thanks for their efforts. Just ask them about John McEnroe or Jimmy

Connors! No love lost there — they have a fierce dislike for many umpires! And it shows, unfortunately.

I was brought up on the philosophy that the 'man in white is always right,' and that's the way it should be — otherwise why have them at all?

With the likes of John 'Superbrat' McEnroe and Jimmy Connors still ranting and raving their way around the tennis courts of the world, it's amazing they've still got people willing to be subjected to excessive badgering and abuse at umpires and linesmen!

Now don't get me wrong, tennis isn't the only game to have its umpiring and personality problems. How would you like to be a soccer referee? No thanks. They take their life into their hands each time they walk onto the pitch in front of the sometimes very volatile crowds.

It's not uncommon to hear of soccer players being banned for life, because of unruly and violent behaviour! I think my old mate and former fast bowling sensation Jeff Thomson upset a soccer referee at the age of 14. So that was the end of a brief career in the round ball game — Thommo got life!

From that point onwards Thommo began to take his frustrations out on batsmen and not umpires . . . although occasionally he's questioned their eyesight and ability to count.

Robin Bailhache the former Test cricket umpire often relates the story about Thommo asking him, "How many balls?" Robin's answer was, "three."

And Thommo's reply, "Is that three gone or three to go?"

Not bad in a six-ball over . . . you've got to remember bowling fast is a thinking man's game!

One of my favourite umpire stories is about Col Edgar, the well respected South Australian Test umpire.

It should be mentioned that cricket is both a mental and physical game with players having to stand for hours under the hot blazing summer sun.

Concentration is essential for success, and breaks in play occur only every two hours. Now if a player is suffering from an upset stomach or nature is calling then — just call on the 12th man. But what if you're an umpire . . . no such luck, they've got to just grin and bear it! Not an easy assignment — depending on the degree of desperation.

Well, exactly that happened in a Test match at the MCG. Col must have taken some sort of bait at lunch — no offence to the MCC caterers — they've always been great. Because after standing in position for about 25 minutes he began suffering with excruciating stomach pains. And he was getting no sympathy from either the batsmen or the fielding side — wickets just weren't falling.

After an hour of increasing pain and intense concentration — he dared not relax the quivering muscles in his buttocks — Col realised he was in real trouble. "If a wicket doesn't fall soon," he thought, "I could disgrace myself and spend a very uncomfortable afternoon standing out here."

Well, the black-trousered umpire was in luck, a wicket did fall, clean bowled.

Somehow Col summoned all his initiative and raced headlong down the wicket towards the shattered set of stumps before his partner at square leg could get there. His only thought was to get off the ground as quickly as possible to relieve the pain.

Without hesitation he uprooted the off stump and waved to the dressing room area, indicating a broken stump.

It was a long journey of griping agony as he hobbled and hopped his way towards the players' gate at the MCG . . . almost passing the dismissed batsman.

With relief almost in sight, through the white players' gate arrived Arnie Beitzel, the dressing room attendant, showing off a brand new stump in his hand for all the spectators to see.

Col's face, already contorted by pain and concentration on making the finishing line, went an ashen green color. Run out by his own team and how!

Umpires have to be resourceful. My dad 'Big Max', often used to talk of the days when he too turned to umpiring. They were days of excitement, some intimidation and much humour.

As a member of the country football umpiring panel, each week he was despatched to unlikely outposts.

He soon learned that trickery and corruption have no bounds. In the earliest stages of his umpiring career he was offered a bribe to manipulate the game. The pay-off was to have been two truck loads of potatoes, all the apples he required and for good measure, the title to an orchard!

Needless to say Big Max was gravely affronted but he'd been taught a valuable lesson.

Then there was another occasion when he did receive fruit and vegetables for his troubles. He copped the lot when the crowd turned sour after a team called Plenty had lost for the first time in two years by a margin of two points against Maydena at the New Norfolk ground.

Every vegetable known on the island, and a vast quantity of rotten eggs, were hurled at him and his colleagues at the end of the match. They'd also let all four tyres down on his zappy little army green, 1950 Ford Prefect. He just had to cop the lot while he slowly pumped up each tyre.

After another match at Molesworth he was hoisted shoulder high by players and officials. "I didn't think I went that well," a beaming Big Max yelled to the crowd beneath him. "You didn't. We're going to chuck you in the bloody creek," said one of the wits in the milling throng of people.

Then came a match at remote Woodsdale in central Tasmania. Despite appalling weather, the local authorities insisted the match be played. All other games in the competition had been abandoned.

In a bid to combat the extreme cold, every player wore a balaclava. They were reasonably effective, but the old man found it impossible to distinguish one player from another. As it was, identification was almost impossible as no cotton jumpers had been available and the players wore numbers crudely papered on various items of clothing deemed appropriate for the occasion. When torrential rain thudded down, the numbers were washed away.

As play was confined to the centre of the sloppy ground for most of the day — there were only four scoring shots for the afternoon — players on each goal line were rendered redundant and spent most of their time huddling under lean-to cattle sheds at the adjacent showgrounds.

All that my umpiring dad could look forward to was his 25-shilling fee for controlling the only match played in the state on that day and a wash with hot water from two 44-gallon drums which had been bubbling for most of the afternoon. He was also keen to warm the cockles of his heart by consuming a couple of saveloys at the rather informal post match assembly.

But he quickly lost his appetite when he saw the saveloys being tossed into the washing water. That's life!

So as you can see it's not all beer and skittles being an umpire, but without them, we haven't got a game. Let's encourage more people to be umpires by respecting them as people.

Now, they won't always be right, but then who is?

The umpire? Oh, he's hangin' about the place.

Caught out by a lizard

'HE DIDN'T KNOW WHICH TROUSER LEG TO HEAD FOR'

As a game, cricket has many facets and many different sorts of participants. When I was a teenager I played the limited over game later developed by Kerry Packer and packaged for TV as one-day cricket.

We only played 21 overs a side in the Hobart Midweek Turf Competition but that was usually enough to produce some unforgettable games.

My old man used to captain a mob from the Liquor Trades and I'll never forget the day that my dad, or 'Big Max' as he was known in the trade, asked a team from the Tramways Board to bat first. No flies on the old man . . . only three Trammies had turned up!

The obvious advantage was to only have to bowl out two batsmen — all out for 2 they were!

Not a huge total to chase so our astute leader decided to allow one of our 'new boys' to open the batting . . . a cheeky young fellow from the big smoke in Melbourne.

He strode to the wicket like a proud peacock in his pure white bri-nylon business shirt and tight fitting, white jeans, but that was just the beginning — he had his batting gloves on inside out. I couldn't believe a man could be so dumb — the green rubber spikes were on the inside of his hands.

I doubt if he'd ever played cricket in his life. So, there he stood, unlike Geoffrey Boycott in every facet of his stance, squinting at the overweight tram conductor who was standing some 155 metres away at the head of his run.

Still we thought our imposter might still have a chance, considering the others only had three men.

Unfortunately for our not so competent No. 1 batsman, he experienced the dreaded 'death rattle' — his stumps cart-wheeled out of the ground, first ball!

Still prepared to gamble and needing three runs to win, a part-time barman, Fred, was given the key job of batting first wicket down.

It was all over in a hurry as Fred belted the second delivery away behind square leg for a boundary. Big Max declared his innings closed at 1 for 4 and the Tramway lads were forced to bat again.

A bonus for the trammies — a latecomer had just walked into the ground to watch the game, but had no gear.

Between the two teams he was given various oddments, and although being plentiful in size, he was dressed and ready to bat.

The Tramways were soon in trouble against the accurate, hostile bowling of Max Walker Senior . . . he was not a pretty sight as he charged into bowl.

Then, suddenly, a long blue-tongued lizard appeared from nowhere! The reptile must have emerged from a watering hole . . . he looked friendly enough and judging by the amount of paint on his back, he was! But tell that to the Trammie, it appeared he was terrified of anything creepy crawly.

The umpire threw his white bowler's hat on top of the problem . . . only to see the hat move slowly up the wicket like a man in a trench. That was humorous enough, but what followed was even better.

One of our fieldsman picked up the hat and beckoned to the frightened batsman to come and have a look . . . "No"! he yelled.

Now that reply was a red rag to a bull, and only served to encourage the playful team-mate of mine.

Then the unexpected happened . . . just when our Tramway friend agreed to have a closer inspection, our little 'blue-tongue' lurched forward out of the umpire's hat and lobbed onto the terrified opponent's shirt. Quick as a flash, claws was spread and he began to climb up the man's clothing but was rejected as flaying arms frightened him. So a change of heart and direction for the lizard — head for terra firma.

But because the borrowed trousers were too big around the belly and the batsman had to wear braces, the lizard disappeared towards the crotch. Needless to say everyone collapsed laughing.

The batter's eyes bulged to the sensations of four tiny legs clambering so near to his crown jewels. All the lizard was looking for was a way out, but no doubt he'd come to the fork in the road and didn't know which trouser leg to head for.

At this stage the warrior in white was frantically kicking his legs up in the air while lying on his back in the middle of the pitch. My old man was out of control with laughter!

Finally the shaken lizard emerged from a gaping fly with the help of the wicketkeeper's gloves. Then he was successfully taken to a culvert at the edge of the ground.

On with the game . . . I can't remember what the score finished up at but believe me it was one hell of a game — ask the shaken trammie.

From that point on, that poor fella was nicknamed 'Goanna' — and he made a duck, too!

Going Crackers over a Meal

'IT WAS A MATTER OF PUSHING ONWARD, EVER ONWARD'

Three huge drops of blood made an interesting abstract pattern as they splashed quietly into the bowl of cream of chicken soup!

My team-mate, Peter 'Crackers' Keenan, had managed to get his nose broken earlier in the afternoon, while playing football — it was a bitter brawling encounter between our team Melbourne and Essendon.

Judging by the swelling and the exaggerated kink in Crackers' more

She couldn't help but notice the three rapidly spreading blobs of blood in my mate's bowl.

than ample nose, Essendon not only won the match, but they also won the fight!

Nevertheless, our weekly after-match ritual of getting together was now well underway — win, lose or draw, it was always good for the team spirit and morale.

Honestly, Crackers Keenan is not a pretty bloke at the best of times, in fact I'm sure his head was chiselled out of granite — now his recently busted beak didn't help.

Sitting opposite the huge, macho ruckman was the wife of one of Melbourne's most respected businessmen.

The businessman's blue Rolls-Royce was parked outside the restaurant and his other half was dressed in splendor — blue-rinse hairdo, bright red lipstick, enormous diamond sparklers hanging from each ear-lobe and several dead foxes draped across her pale shoulders.

The beautifully manicured lady couldn't help but notice the three rapidly spreading blobs of blood in my mate's bowl!

But cool as an ice-cube, the big fella looked up, straight across the table, took a deep breath through his partly blocked nose — to stem the flow of blood without having to use his handerkerchief — then confidently plunged his silver spoon deep into the heart of his soup.

At the same time the elegant lady's cheeks became ashen-grey. Yes, she'd guessed it, Crackers was going to eat it — blood and all. How could he?

There he was Peter Pius Paul Keenan, fresh from the famous Catholic college at Kilmore — Assumption — dressed in a 'closing down' sale-priced, purple polyester suit, pink shirt, wide Paisley tie matching his even wider lapels, white socks and an outrageous pair of black pointy-toed shoes. It was clear to see our man was right at the fore-front of early 70's fashion, even though he was sitting on his taste buds.

Within seconds he'd swallowed the first spoonful of blood-stained soup, with much disgust all round — it really was a sickening sight.

His 'friend' across the soup bowl, waited only three more spoonfuls before leaving the party . . . but as Crackers said, "Where's she gone, the night's only just begun?"

But so too had the meal . . . not much more was eaten by anybody after the starter from Crackers!

Funny how every detail of some meals just seem to become etched into one's mind.

When I first came to Melbourne from Hobart as a teenager to play VFL footy and study architecture at the Royal Melbourne Institute of Technology, I must admit some of my own home-cooked meals were pretty ordinary . . . something I bet many students can relate to.

Not much money, not much time and no expertise in the art of cooking — if it didn't come in a can, I was in trouble. I even had trouble boiling water.

One night the kitchen cupboard was bare — all that remained was a box of spaghetti; it had been there for nearly six months and I just wasn't sure how to cook it. But no guts no glory . . . I had a go!

Into the saucepan full of boiling water went the long, tender splinters of spaghetti, some breaking off, and some bending in the heated water. Soon it was limp and white as spaghetti should look.

Now it was ready to eat . . . the mouth watered at the thought of spaghetti Bolognaise. One minor problem though — what about the meat sauce?

I'd completely forgotten and time was moving on . . . only one thing to do — go for the Heinz Big Red tomato sauce.

It certainly lacked meat, but I loved tomato sauce anyway, so everything was fine!

Although cold, bottled sauce on steaming, over-cooked spaghetti wasn't the norm, it tasted 'fine' to me . . . well, after all that effort, I wasn't about to turn around and criticise my own creation.

I sat down to a pretty bland old meal, but I got through it . . . even had some leftovers in the simmering pot.

So why not have some sweets, like macaroni, I thought, and I did!

It was just a matter of cutting up the remaining, rubbery strands of spaghetti into tiny lengths, adding some sugar for sweetness and topping it off with a scoop of vanilla ice cream. The taste at best, was different.

When I think back to those formative years as a student, I wonder how I ever got through . . . but as for all goal-oriented young people it was just a matter of pushing onward, ever onward, no matter what the conditions were.

A very good friend of mine through the RMIT days, Dal Wild, had accommodation in a trendy house shared with four other students — three guys and a girl.

Dal's room was a wonderfully arty expression of the man at the time. He used a British flag as a bedspread.

Light for the room came from a lonely filament globe trapped in a sawn-off champagne bottle. His drafting desk (a secondhand door), was neatly supported on concrete building blocks. The desk was beneath an elevated bed built of 'recovered' timber from a nearby demolition site. The only access to this almighty place of slumber was up a rope ladder. I can only say that Dal had many a hair-raising climb up the primitive stairs after a big night on the red wine.

Still, it was a great meeting place for the spontaneous exchange of ideas . . . we had many a feed of fish and chips on the old pine table out the back of the house.

But one day we arrived home unexpectedly to find one of his flatmates cooking — an Asian student named Jonathan. He was preparing a very different meal.

Much to our horror, he had Dal's pet goldfish out of the glass bowl and into the frying pan. It was such a pathetic sight — these two tiny little fish, no more than one inch long, sizzling away in a great big black frying pan.

If we hadn't been so angry I supposed we would have offered him some of our chips, because there was no way known the two sardine-like pieces of fish would be a full meal.

For Jonathan that experience was sadly just the beginning of the end. The writing was on the wall. He went completely off the rails and had a nervous breakdown — too much pressure to succeed from his parents back home.

But before he left, he chased Susie, the only female lodger, out of the shower, naked, and into the street, brandishing a very large, super sharp carving knife.

So much for being a student. It takes all kinds, but it sure was fun.

Turning Red at the Sight of Pink

'*I ENDED UP DRAFTING WITH AN ALARM CLOCK ON MY DESK*'

I don't believe in ghosts, but I'm worried about the effects the 'grey ghosts', as we call our parking attendants in Melbourne, are having on fellow motorists. Just leave your car unguarded for a fleeting moment and they'll slap a pink sticker on your windscreen.

Try and look one in the eye while they're frantically scribbling out the details on their ever-ready pad and you'll be disappointed.

The way in which they go about their job is unbelievable!

On a Test match weekend at the MCG when thousands of mums, dads and kids are out enjoying the sporting occasion — the grey ghosts see it as an excuse to work overtime. Honestly, many of these characters give more signatures away than Dennis Lillee would autographs!

The big difference being Lillee used to give his loopy signature away free of charge — all you had to do was ask! Now our silently lurking friends never wait to be asked and the average cost is about $30.

Imagine if all their collections went to charity? By the way, where does all that loot go? Certainly not to fit 'em out with new, brighter and easier to spot uniforms. As a group of people, I've never met a more solemn lot.

They gave a serve to a good friend of mine who just happened to have put in a particularly big weekend. Yes, my mate had been to a Saturday/Sunday party and after drinking absolute truckloads, he flaked in the back seat of his car. That was late on Sunday night.

By the time he woke up at lunchtime on Tuesday (allowing for a little exaggeration) he couldn't see out of the front window for parking fines.

You'd reckon the attendant might have shown some commonsense after the third ticket and asked a straight-forward question like, "Are you all right mate?" or "How long do you intend staying here? Your meter's expired."

Obviously he needed to accomplish his quota for the day.

Many years ago in Tasmania, my dad had a hot-headed foreman working for him. The project was to replace a jeweller's shop window and fittings which had been broken into by vandals and looted.

The job looked like taking about six or seven hours and it was necessary to park right outside the jewellery shop to save lugging heavy equipment in and out of the shop.

The foreman's name was Brian, and he didn't stop moaning about the amount of damage the vandals had caused to the shop front. The same man was a brilliant craftsman and soon got down to the nitty gritty of refurbishing the broken shelves, the shattered windowpanes and the display cases inside the shop. Before he knew it, lunchtime was only minutes away.

Much to Brian's disgust, the sign 'MEN AT WORK' had failed to have much impact. Two parking notices were stuck to the cracked window of his ex-army jeep. Two similar items decorated my old man's windscreen.

The ambitious young parking attendant didn't realise at the time, but booking these 'men at work' he was really playing a dangerous game.

Brian waited and waited for the 'smart alec' who booked him to reappear. No such luck! The blood pressure was rising by the minute . . . veins stood out around his temples as the rage inside increased! Finally he cracked!

Without a second thought, he grabbed the hacksaw from the back of his rusty old jeep. Just as a man about to fell a tree would, he sized up just where to make the cut.

Booking these men was really playing a dangerous game.

In Brian's case, the line of saw-cut needed to be about six inches below the bright red 'expired' sign which now covered the well fed meter's face.

It took him less than five minutes to completely behead the two offending parking meters with his trusty hacksaw blade.

Just a stone's throw away in the middle of busy Elizabeth Street, the Tramways were carrying out repairs to their ageing tracks. Deep gashes in the bitumen road's surface exposed the orange clay below. It didn't take long for the two dead meter heads to end up on a big pile of dirt just in front of a slowly moving bulldozer. The driver was oblivious to their presence but a curious crowd had grown to watch the blade of the powerful bulldozer bury its two victims.

I'd have loved to check out the expression on the young parking attendant when he did finally arrive on the scene.

Still I guess they're expected to cope with a whole variety of reactions — mostly aggressive.

Apart from football umpires, these parking meter watchdogs must be just about the most verbally doused people in town.

When I worked in the city as an architect, I too used to run the daily gauntlet of playing the meters. It meant checking all four tyres every couple of hours for tell-tale yellow chalk marks, identifying just how long the car had been in the area.

It was possible to roll the car back or forward to cover the mark or remove the marks. Even sandpaper was used.

Needless to say a difficult problem on the drawing board generally cost the price of a parking ticket. I ended up drafting with an alarm clock on my desk.

I'm a great believer in natural justice. Sure enough, one day I saw a parking attendant reach his day of reckoning.

Right before my eyes from the second storey window of an adjacent terrace house, I witnessed the entire contents of a bed pan being emptied over an unsuspecting parking man. One, two, even three tickets the old lady could handle, but not four! That was the one that lit the fuse, and SPLASH! Not a happy ending to that story.

I've noticed motorists prowling around looking for the impossible park, change their tack if a parking attendant was present. They'd wait for the officer of the local council to bend over in order to mark the tyre . . . the driver would speed up level with the car in question, then hoot loudly. That was generally reckoned to be enough to take a few years off the parking attendant's life.

Mates of mine, and I'm not proud of them, have even left a handful of tacks under the back wheel of an unattended motorcycle belonging to a lurking attendant.

I know they're only doing their job but gee, they can be irritating to say the least.

Just a few weeks ago I left my car in a loading zone — I'm on a non-commercial registration — to drop off two pairs of trousers and pick up two jackets at the dry cleaners.

There is no way known I was gone more than four minutes, yet there it was pasted at 45 degrees on the passenger side window and not a grey ghost in sight — disappeared into thin air.

I don't have to tell you how I felt. It sure put up the price of dry cleaning.

It takes all sorts, but it must take a lot of soul searching to finally agree to be a parking officer. Whatever the attraction, it can't be for the money.

Well, that's done my dash. From now on, I've got no hope in the parking stakes. They'll probably put a tail on me just to get even! I reckon they're well in front already.

Chapter Four

A COUNTRY RICH IN HUMOUR

Real cricket in the red dust

'A WICKETKEEPER HAD BROKEN HIS HAND TRYING TO REMOVE THE BAILS'

The day was March 13, 1985. I'm not superstitious but ... I woke up with a start as my head bounced off the passenger door window. Coming straight at our car at 120 kmh, was a yellow and black, diamond-shaped sign post saying: FLOODWAY.

In that split second of opening my eyes it was terrifyingly obvious that the car in which I was a passenger was not on the black bitumen stuff where it ought to have been!

There was no question and no escape — we were definitely going to crash into the post. In fact we hit it dead centre and it buckled like a tooth-pick. The next few seconds were horrific to say the least.

The metal sign crashed into the windscreen right in front of my eyes. Splinters of glass flew everywhere as the window crazed like a spider's web.

My door began to open but I pulled against it. The potentially lethal sign somehow didn't get through the window but ricocheted over the bonnet as the car began to spin.

I momentarily felt like Steve McQueen filming *Bullitt* but what a waste — there were no cameras.

Finally, the car came to a standstill after completing about eight loop-the-loops over the red dust and short-tufted scrub grass. My arm was aching from holding the passenger's door shut against the force of gravity. At this stage I had stopped screaming expletives!

Lionel, the driver, looked ashen. the colour returned, except for the knuckles of his fingers tightly gripping the steering wheel. A deadly silence prevailed.

Yes, we were very lucky to be alive after leaving the road at such a speed and not rolling the vehicle.

We were on our way to a speaking engagement at Leigh Creek football and cricket clubs, some five hours driving out of Adelaide.

As I looked back to the road, I could see the mangled signpost about 100 metres away pointing to the sky like a scorpion's tale.

I also noticed a two-metre wide concrete culvert or waterway just 10 metres away from where the car had stopped spinning ... again I thought of all the possibilities. We sure were lucky!

Within minutes a big blue Range Rover came to an abrupt halt in a cloud of dust and two guys, Dave and Leon, rushed over to see what had happened.

As I found out later, it wasnt't the first time these two blokes had stopped to lend a helping hand. "Anyone hurt?" they shouted, scampering quickly towards Lionel and myself.

All four of us did a complete lap of honor, inspecting the white, late model Ford Falcon. By the time we had completed the enlightening walk, I noticed Leon staring at me.

He thought he'd seen me somewhere before but the penny didn't drop quickly for him. Then again, I guess he thought, 'what's Dennis Lillee or maybe Max Walker doing in the region of the iron triangle? No it couldn't be him!!!' After all, it was a long way from the turf of the MCG, eh?

I felt some pain in my left hand, blood was dripping from my fingertips. Lionel said: "Max, are you all right?" then Leon, the short, yet enormously wide man, smiled with recognition.

He must have been 23 stone (convert that to metric if you can), dressed for the trip in blue singlet and shorts, topped off with an unpressed khaki shirt.

His thin mate Dave's trousers told the story of his trade, such was the amount of grease on them. In many ways together they appeared like the original Laurel and Hardy team — Leon providing the laughs while Dave was the straight man.

Boy, were we glad to see them as we stood in front of the crumpled bonnet and watched a tell-tale spiral of steam come from a damaged radiator.

All our efforts to prise open the bonnet failed until a crowbar was produced. Watching Lionel perspiring profusely as he worked, any hope of the car being driveable was quickly diminishing.

Then, the sound of air brakes punctuated the air. We looked up and saw a magnificent road train pull up, chrome shining. It is moments like these that you reflect on the world and think there really are some tremendous people around. The first two vehicles to come our way had stopped and couldn't do enough for us.

The two-way radio inside the cabin was of great assistance in calling the local Ford dealer in Quovis. Lionel stayed with his car on the roadside and waited while it was agreed that I should continue to Leigh Creek.

As luck would have it, Dave and Leon were going to Leigh Creek to put some heavy earthmoving equipment on the train to Port Augusta.

Some 100 kilometres down the road it became clear why Lionel wanted to stay with his car. My new friends described many an incident of cars being stripped whilst the owner went for petrol or the car had been left after a crash.

Dave had learnt the lesson in an unusual way. He'd just completed jacking up his car to change a flat tyre, while his mate looked on from his own car parked just in front. A late model sports car pulled up behind both of them. A guy in trendy gear got out, raced over to Dave and said: "Let's not be greedy, eh? You take the back tyres and I'll take the front two!" Dave couldn't believe his ears as he shouted, "It's my bloody car!"

This saw the trendy man hightail it off into the distance at extremely high speed.

When we arrived at our destination, words didn't seem to be enough to express how grateful I was for Dave and Leon's help. Maybe one day I will be able to reciprocate.

After a quick shower, my room at the canteen soon became the venue for some cricket stories. This time I was listening . . . fascinated by some real red dust Australian tales of bat and ball.

The match was an annual event played for the fourth time between Wilpoorinna, a team provided by wealthy station owners, the Litchfield family, and of course the Leigh Creek boys, selected from those still standing and available.

I hadn't heard of the Wilpoorinna Sporting Complex before — this apparently was where the game was played.

An early disappointment was the fact that 'Two Step Terry' the president of LCFC would be unavailable due to poisoning — it's not known what sort but I doubt if you'd need a medical degree to guess.

The wicket itself was a four feet wide concrete test strip laid by an inexperienced local. From end-to-end there was no less than a six-inch fall — talk about the ridge at Lords!

A boundary line was achieved by dragging around a fallen log behind a horse about 65 yards from the concrete pitch, thus forming a groove. The outfield itself consisted of Leigh Creek mulch or basically a lot of rocks and no grass — no curator needed at this ground.

The main pavilion was two horse drays and a canvas secured only by logs — this provided limited shade considering temperatures regularly hit 45 deg. C in this part of Australia. In the outer I'm told were just a couple of EH Holdens with their own tent outhouses and well-stocked coolers.

The stumps fascinated me — firmly set in concrete and made from one piece of flat metal — and the metal bails were welded on! This had been a contentious point because in an earlier game a wicketkeeper had broken his hand trying to remove the bails! There was some talk of removing the bails with a hack saw blade!

Beside each of the fieldsman's feet it is not unusual to spot a stubby marking his position. The general idea with these is to break your mate's stubby with a rock before he can drink it.

Three cork cricket balls are used per innings because of wear and tear caused by the rocky surroundings. Fieldsmen just don't dive in these games as the possibility of the ball ricocheting into your face from the rocks is very real. As they say in Leigh Creek, you can either be a dead hero or a squib.

Because of the type of balls used, the bats themselves are covered with black polypipe melted by oxy-torches and shrunk around the face of the bat — most bats weigh around 4 lbs. You'd need forearms like Rod Marsh to lift one, eh?

Casualties were a common occurrence, the worst being 'Kempie' who had only just returned to Wilpoorinna. He was on 10 looking for a second run, after a particularly fast single, when he ran smack bang into George

Menangitus, a new school teacher in the town. The final outcome was 10 stitches in the chin. And he'd just driven 600 km from Mt Barker to play. Then he drove 80 km to hospital and desperately drove the return 80 km to the club only to find the beer off and the club shut! You can't beat bad luck.

One interesting dismissal entered into the score sheet on the back of a piece of cardboard was: 'Thommo' caught Tort (wicketkeeper) bowled Bouncie (swing bowler). Score — not many.

I should mention that Leigh Creek won this 1985 encounter for the first time in four years after scoring 124 in 20 overs. All that raised $1500 for the Isolated Children's and Parents Association and a great day was had by all.

That's what I call real cricket — no coloured gear and flash $5 million lighting.

The View from the Top
'MY BODY HAD NOT SUFFERED THIS TYPE OF TREATMENT FOR QUITE A WHILE'

Many great sporting coaches have used the comparison of climbing a mountain to success in the sporting arena. It is often stated that there is a lot of room half way up the mountain and that is very true! Similarly, the 'view' from just above the half way mark is pretty good.

Now, let's talk about the top of the mountain! From here, the view is nothing short of magnificent . . . . maybe that's why there is not much room at the top?

In fact, it's probably very difficult to put into words just what the view is like, or how it feels to have conquered the summit, whatever it may be! But certainly to stand there alone on a dais or even with a few worthy mates, and to experience that fleeting moment of triumph, is something that money can't buy.

Ask anyone who has ever won an Olympic gold medal or world championship. Speak to members of a football premiership team; they will all agree it was hard work, but well worth the effort.

For most of these champions, the winning and success was both the journey and the destination — not just the end result!

Well, I didn't climb the mountain, but I did climb a rock. And it was a big one too — Ayers Rock in Central Australia.

As I stood atop that huge hunk of rock, wind blasting in my face and hair ruffling my forehead, I felt just like Sir Edmund Hillary, the New Zealand mountain climber, must have felt when he conquered Everest. I had achieved what I set out to do. So you can understand I was more than just a little happy about it all — exhilarated to say the least!

A small metal plaque is located at the highest point on the crown of the massive spiritual rock which the Aboriginals call Uluru.

This point is some 348.7 metres above the surrounding desert plains. Like all before me, I signed my name in a rather flimsy exercise book which amazed me by its ability to remain intact in the wind.

Before I describe the actual assault on just about the most famous rock in the world, maybe I should explain exactly what I was doing at Ayers Rock.

The Sheraton Hotel at the Yulara Tourist Resort, NT, was the venue for the Digital Equipment Corporation's South Pacific Region Conference for 1985. I was invited to chair the conference and, needless to say, it was a very enriching experience for all concerned — some 200 'digits' and a few other lucky individuals.

One thought about the visit that made me smile a lot, was the question of laundry. We were told not to leave our laundry bags outside our doors because . . . wait for it! Yes, dingoes were likely to take them away if there was even the slightest scent of B.O. around and I can testify there was plenty of that around.

Here we were in a fabulous international class hotel and our biggest problem was whether or not a dingo was going to pinch our laundry bag. Incredible! But I must admit I did find some footprints within 10 metres of the building which looked a lot like dingo prints . . . Go on, ask me what a dingo print looks like! Well, I don't know really, but it makes a good story doesn't it?

The special systems group I was with was part of a very successful computer company — the Design and Build Group.

Yes, you won't believe it, but after a lot of blood, sweat and tears, these guys were able to set up a video terminal and keyboard right on top of the rock. Obviously, it was a battery powered unit, connected to a computer at the base of the rock by radio.

The theory being, each time a successful challenge was mounted, the conquering person's name was personally entered into the keyboard, checked on the monitor and transmitted to the printer at car park level, thus documenting the climb in the form of a two-colour certificate.

I really do admire those guys who lugged the very heavy battery keyboard, inverter and monitor all the way up to the rock's peak — not only are they fit, they're bloody mad!

To make their task easier, they used the aid of darkness to knock off the porter's two wheel trolley, as well as his card table . . . that could even still be up there, eh?

The world record for the journey is approximately 12 minutes. One of the digits from NZ did it in 18 minutes. But then again there are a lot of hills in NZ! I think the average time was more like 90 minutes — many scenic stops on the way! Well, that's what they're saying, and I'm not calling them liars.

It should also be stated that more than a handful of tourists have made Ayers Rock their last stopover — they died in their attempt.

I'm sure this fact was firmly entrenched in my mind when I set off up the very steep rock face — the direction of travel marked by a long line of ant-like figures above, clingly tightly to a chain which threaded its way through many uprights at approximately three metre intervals. This was, to many climbers a life support system as both blood pressure and colour in the cheeks rose simultaneously.

The fitter a person is, the quicker their so-called 'second wind' arrives or the heartburn stops. Well, I reckon I'd climbed the first 100 metres of an almost vertical rock face — I'm prone to exaggerate, but gee, it was steep. Anyway, my heartburn was getting worse, not less! My thighs were aching just above the knees, and the meat pie I had for morning tea was just starting to surface!

I tried using an old sporting trick of mine . . . when in pain think of something else. You know, I really tried, but for the life of me I couldn't think of anything to take the place of the overall pain. Needless to say my body had not suffered this sort of treatment for quite a while.

Then, at one-third-of-the-way-up point, the changing point in my outlook occurred . . . it was like a breath of fresh air. I saw a little old lady coming down the rock face on my right. She had a big beaming smile on her face. I couldn't resist the temptation to ask her age. "Sixty three," she said without hesitation. My lungs filled with air and my mind with positive, lively thoughts.

Once over the bull-nosed section of the rock called 'chicken rock', we'd reached the point of no return. It was easy from here as I followed my better than suntanned nose and the white line in front of me. I wonder how many gallons of paint it took to paint that dotted line . . . either that, or there are some pretty big pigeons around! What a job, lugging several gallons of white paint up a hill like that . . . and probably with the lid off ready for a tip or two of the brush!

Before I reached the high point of the rock, I took every opportunity to view the Olgas in the background — nestled on the horizon like a huge sleeping lizard.

I bet you didn't know that Ayers Rock could be placed inside the cluster called the Olgas without displacing a rock — well neither did I, until a local told me!

It was one thing to go up and another to get back down again. Before I was half way down the steep incline, I had worn both back pockets from my jeans and one side of my leather wallet. There was a gaping hole in two $20 bills! Another couple of long and abrasive slides like that and it could have been a very cheeky descent!

Whereas the pressure on the way up belonged to my thighs and Achilles tendons, the knees and toes copped plenty on the way down. I could tell we were making progress, if only slowly, because the 'hundreds and

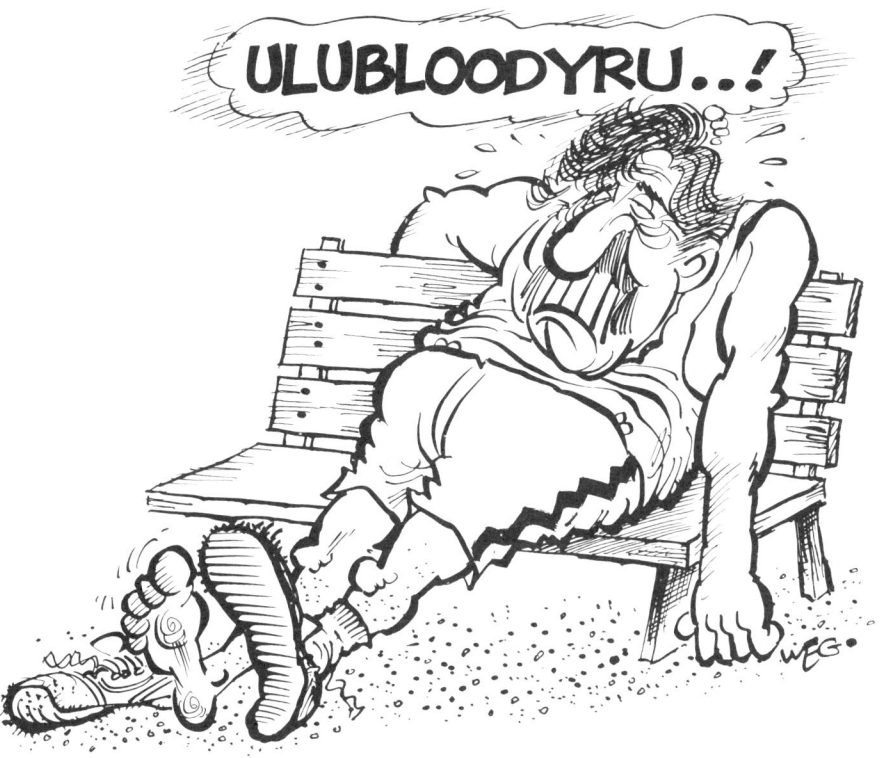

thousands' sprinkled in the car park were gradually looking more like cars and four-wheel drive vehicles. And the gum trees at ground level no longer looked like grass anymore.

"Hooray!" We made it to the ground. My legs began shaking gently, like jelly, in protest at finally walking on a flat surface again.

What a satisfying day . . . The computer spat out my certificate, a few more last minute photographs and back to the serious business of chairing the conference at Yulara.

Pleasures of the Ettamogah Pub
'IT WAS TOO EARLY FOR A BEER . . .'

I put my eye to the camera with a view to capturing yet another memorable image. The Andamooka drive-in theatre was something else! Unique, would be a fair description.

Behind me stood an opal miner, forcefully shaking his right index finger at me. The guy was dressed in an unbuttoned check shirt and dusty denim trousers. His dark eyes were set just above very high cheek bones. It was obvious from his accent that he was of European parentage.

I wasn't too sure what to do . . . continue photographing and ignore my 'friend' or turn around and face him like a man. In fact the whole scenario had a touch of the old western movies about it: The sun was quickly setting in the west, drenching the red, dusty landscape in a beautiful golden haze. All we needed was a pistol each and a duel to the death would have eventuated!

I decided to face him like a man. I immediately put down my Canon camera and walked towards him believing that I wasn't trespassing on his property.

His next words surprised me, "You must be the famous cricket player?" On hearing this I thought I had a chance of avoiding a fight! But he still hadn't smiled and I wasn't game to try one of my sure-fire one liners on him just yet.

He beckoned me over and said, "Do ya wanna have a look at how an Andamooka bachelor lives?"

I accepted immediately because, after all, I didn't want to offend the man. Later, with two travelling companions, Graham Charlton and Brian Tolhurst, we disappeared inside the rather basic fibro-cement structure our new mate called 'home'.

Introductions were made all round and the possibility of a nice cold beer looked very good. Especially as we'd been travelling for about five hours on the dusty, corrugated road leading to Andamooka a long, long way north-west of Adelaide.

Slobo Pavlovic was his name and he admitted knowing absolutely nothing about the game of cricket, but he did profess to know everything there was to know about soccer.

Tucked below the modest exterior of his home was a lavish entertainment area protected from the cold of night and the searing daytime heat. The mood was set off by several posters of young Australian womanhood!

After several beers, it was time to move on, but not before we met Slobo's mate, Willy, another soccer fanatic. They both needed written proof that the 'cricket player' had actually been in their dug-out. We just happened to have a couple of my posters in the boot of the car. Both of them were ecstatic, as if they'd just discovered a large deposit of black opal on their claim.

It is always great to have a chance meeting with fellas like Slobo and his mate. You then get a real picture of what places such as Andamooka are like, without the tinsel.

I had to wait until sun up to get a second picture of the drive-in because darkness prevailed outside. The temperature had dropped dramatically under a clear sky and the Southern Cross looked as clear as I've ever seen it among the millions of other brilliant yellow lights in the black canopy above us.

Back on tour in the morning, what better way to begin a day than pull up at the first pub along the way? It was barely 7 a.m. when we discovered what turned out to the 'the smallest pub in the world' — The Ettamogah Pub; licensee W. 'Bill' MacDougall.

It truly was a sight to behold and a signwriter's dream.

The actual construction cost of what really was an exercise in basic, organic architecture, was a very reasonable $7.50. Believe me it was a bargain. Some of the signs adorning the main structure, a rusty corrugated iron cube on a concrete slab, had come from as far afield as North America. There was one suggesting *'Emergency Snow Street, No Parking when snow exceeds 2 inches'*.

All I can say is that if two inches of snow fell in the vicinity of Bill's hotel, he would want to be wearing more than he was at the time we sprung him.

Admittedly it was a pretty odd hour to call in. What hair old Bill has managed to maintain can't remember when it last saw a comb and looked like the direct hit by a large bolt of lightning.

The face had character, set as it was among the creases and camouflaged by an untamed silver beard.

We had interrupted his morning constitution. Our first sight of him was a furry arm and leg and a blue Royal Flying Doctor tee shirt. I thought, 'Strewth what have we got here — the Nullarbor Nymph?' Obviously too old, not pretty and in the wrong part of the continent.

We very quickly made friends with the shake of a hand. He apologised for not meeting us in the foyer of his eye-catching hotel. I felt guilty — we should have apologised to him, although I guess that far away from civilisation, the morning paper would not be delivered with breakfast, eh?

As we waited inside for the portable hotplate to boil the kettle, my eyes wandered with interest to the array of collectables he had on display. The manner in which they were arranged suggested an eye for detail. Maybe the oldtimer had an artistic background?

It was too early for a beer, so we accepted a piping hot cup of tea together with fresh teddy bear biscuits. How could anyone have fresh teddy bear biscuits out here? They were fantastic.

Then, the oldtimer told us of his involvement in the Royal Flying Doctor Service over many years. He went on to say that all proceeds made from his pub went to the service. Over three years he raised $11,000, $14,000 and $17,000 respectively. Fantastic effort for a one-man show, eh?

We were offered a go in his 'lucky dip' before we left. Brian won a tea-towel. And by winning it meant a chance to be eligible for the TV sitting on top one of the dusty, broken down fridges Bill owned. Without even taking Brian's name or address, Bill said, "Son, I'll notify you if you win it!".

After I'd taken quite a few pictures of Bill, he recalled the time when a Japanese tourist asked if he could take a picture of his wife in bed with Bill. You'd have to have a warped sense of humour to get into bed with Bill, but it sure would make a great picture.

He also admitted listening to my cricket commentaries during the summer — that was after he had just lost his corrugated iron roof for the second time during a cyclone. His makeshift WC ended up on top of it, thus exposing the seating structure straddling an old mining shaft. Not exactly an ensuite with bidet and tiled floor, eh?

I couldn't help but wonder at the motivating forces behind an existence like Bill MacDougall's or Slobo's. What would you do in a place like Andamooka? Maybe go to the drive-in. Hardly any need to take the car. I loved the two speakers, set up on two, rusted 44 gallon drums that made up the projection 'house'.

Everywhere I looked in Andamooka I had to take a picture. I'm pretty certain that some of those rough-hewn, hand-built dwellings and dugout entries housed some pretty exciting accommodation. They were cut into the white kopi soil and sandstone without any visible signs of shoring.

Even the dead were buried beneath a bed of dust on an opalised barren hill top — a bit like 'Boot Hill'! Yet this landscape of mullock heaps and red dust is home for maybe 600 prospectors. I admire their courage and probably in some cases, their hidden wealth.

On our long journey the hierarchy of the animal kingdom was evident even in the most barren areas. Wedgetailed eagles rule supreme, floating high above their territories, surveying their prey. I was even lucky enough to capture a few pics of these beautiful birds of prey, eyeball to eyeball. As I thrust the big lens toward the hooked beak, I wasn't aware of the potential danger. It would have been so easy for the big winged beauty to attack me with devastating results. It certainly helped having a big cheesy grin!

Judging by the number of dead kangaroos on the roadside there was probably no reason for the eagle to attack me! There must have been 100 dead roos counted on the way home. Tragic, because most would have been killed by motor vehicles.

We nearly added to the tally. Four really big fellas decided to cross the road all at once but only three got there safely. We hit the fourth kangaroo a glancing blow at about 110 kmh. We were lucky.

It's easy to see how people have been killed by swerving to miss a roo. And the kangaroo doesn't front for the funeral!

Whatever the risk, the stark beauty of Central Australia and its inhabitants is definitely worth experiencing. Go on . . . make the effort!

Plain sailing for a week

'BOTH SHEETS WERE FULL OF WIND AS WE HEADED FOR THE HORIZON'

Some weeks are better than others but the seven days beginning Friday, October 24, 1985 were magnificent — 168 hours of full on go! Melbourne — Sydney — Melbourne — Airlie Beach — Hamilton Island — Brisbane — Surfers Paradise — Melbourne, and fortunately a late cancellation on a speaking engagement in Adelaide!

Actually, the week-long physical endurance test only happened because my dulcet tones were not required in Adelaide for the Channel 9 coverage of the 1985 Australian Grand Prix.

To be honest, I was disappointed at missing out on the festivities surrounding the inaugural Formula One race in the city of churches ... but by the time my week was over, I was certain I hadn't been short changed!

I was hitting Sydney town early Friday to help my old mate Jeff Thomson launch his frank book called *Thommo Declares* — the life and times of cricket's most colourful larrikin ... and where better to launch it than at the famous Sydney Cricket Ground.

For the man who captured 200 Test wickets and sent the fear of God into many of the world's top batsmen with his lethal catapult deliveries, the SCG represented the scene of some great triumphs.

The SCG was where Thommo began his first class career with NSW and tragically that's where it all ended in an emotional finish to the 1985-86 Sheffield Shield final. The big blond quick's dream of bowing out with the Sheffield Shield under one arm and slab of cans under the other would have been great but you can't win 'em all.

Nevertheless, as he mentions in the book in pretty blunt terms, you can give them one hell of a fright. So for the world's fastest certified bowler (Guinness Book of Records) life was now about to change direction. No less hectic, but now his energies are focused on his rapidly growing landscape business in Brisbane and if I know Thommo, he'll blitz 'em in this arena too.

Unfortunately no time to socialise and share a million tales of yesterday ... off the catch another plane, but not before saying "Hello" to Thommo's mum and dad. Mum said: "Gee, thanks, but you didn't have to say all those nice things about Jeff!"

Thommo appeared from the members' bar with a drink and a typical thank you blast, "Nothing's changed, you're still talking bulldust Tangles!"

Anyway, back to the news desk at Bendigo Street, Richmond, for another sports bulletin on the six o'clock TV news.

Then with the night still very much a pup, off with the make-up. Gee, now I know what women must go through! And it's not good — first the cleanser and I try not to dirty my collar because it'll save time if I don't have to change my shirt. Actually it's only been on for half an hour.

I take off the cleanser with tissue paper ... what a sight! Next, the soap and water. My white collar is still clean, you little beauty! Or is it?

I guess you can't beat bad luck — a tell tale brown make-up stain on my left collar. What would the staff of Westpac think who were already gathered at their training college at Lilydale in Victoria where I am usually first speaker for their 'Time out' training weekends?

So on with a squirt of the underarm and quick knot in the tie. Gee, I've forgotten the moisturiser. No, I'm not a sheila — but I must carry make-up, cleanser and moisturiser in my toiletries.

A fairly heavy-footed drive from GTV-9 lands me in the Westpac carpark in time for the main course — my favorite, Cordon Bleu plus chips.

The banking industry is like any other industry at the moment — very competitive and getting itself in line with new technology. Many people in banking have a lot of unanswered questions about the future floating around in their heads, so for the 20 to 30 who volunteered to take the course, it was the beginning of what I believe is always a very enlightening 48 hours.

After talking to these young people, who had chosen to have a concerned attitude to the future, it was a dash back home to find the household sound asleep.

Unconsciously, I grab my old faithful black suitcase from its pigeon hole and begin to pack my bags . . . the hour is well after midnight and I try to be quiet, like a good room-mate should.

What will I need for four days in Queensland? Certainly no heavy grey suits — it's been a while since I've hit the Sunshine State so my selection of clothes takes a little longer, especially as I'll be spending some time on board a yacht in the Whitsunday Islands.

6.05 a.m.: Saturday, Long Term Carpark, Tullamarine Airport . . . the temperature is around 8 degrees Celsius and is trying to rain . . . I've got a colourful short-sleeved shirt on and my body is covered in goose pimples.

7.00 a.m.: The Ansett plane fires its jets and we taxi down the runway.

10.40 a.m.: It was like walking into a furnace at Proserpine as I crossed the tarmac. Apparently five inches of rain had fallen prior to my arrival and the humidity must have been 100 per cent. By the time I spotted my baggage on the truck, my shirt was wringing wet . . . no amount of underarm will save me now, my skin was looking like a tea strainer.

My contact, Richard Watson, formerly of the South Australian Cricket Association and newly appointed to the Whitsunday Tourism Authority, bundled me into his car (without air-conditioning) and suggested we stop off for a starter on the way to Airlie Beach.

The chosen pub in Proserpine was run by Tom Hill who proudly showed me his latest trophy . . . won by defeating a few other desperate jockeys on wooden rocking horses — not exactly the Melbourne Cup.

Let me tell you it is one of the most original trophies I've ever seen. Yes, here I was holding this stainless steel bedpan mounted on a beautiful piece of polished timber. Just as in the VFL Grand final, the winner gets to savor the victory champagne from the coveted symbol of supremacy. So in this case the spout of the bedpan . . . well that's the way the story goes.

Airlie Beach here I come . . . lunch was to be on a yacht.

A quick change into shorts and thongs and off to sea we went. Before long I was a poor man's John Bertrand standing at the back of the boat with the wheel firmly in my grasp. Both sheets were full of wind as we headed for the horizon.

Bernie Katchor or 'Bernie of the Barrier Reef', as the owner of the beautiful craft that I was now in control of was nicknamed, was pretty impressed with my nautical terminology.

So, sharing the same warped sense of humour when I quizzed him for some direction about where he wanted me to sail, he responded: "Aim for those trees on the island out there!" The problem was there were heaps of islands out ahead and all of them had a healthy covering of trees.

Being a positive thinker, I just imagined I was captain of Australia II and went for broke . . . seaspray in the face, and the odd shout of "tacking" made for a marvellous experience.

I can understand why the red-bearded man with the white floppy hat settled in Shute Harbor and built a business around having fun — Whitsunday Rent-a-Yacht. What a day cruising around the blue/green waters . . . not a phone in earshot, only jovial chatter and a social ale. You've just gotta live longer in this part of the world.

Before we moored our yacht, called *Big Time*, the question of tomorrow arose. "You wouldn't want to go out sailing again tomorrow would ya?" someone asked.

I said, "Can a duck swim?"

And the problem was solved — more sailing. First there was the reason for being in this part of the world — to launch the third book in a series by Ron and Ngaire Gale.

Approximately 50,000 photographs had been looked at before selecting the formats for these wonderfully graphic tributes to our sunny north — the last one simply called *Australia's Whitsundays.*

Some of the photographs are breathtaking, but you can't beat the real thing and I wanted to see for myself.

Snorkelling is something I haven't done much of, so on the Sunday — day two of my epic sailing adventure — I got my big chance. Flippers intact, backwards over the edge with a big splash a la Lloyd Bridges in *Sea Hunt,* the old black and white TV series.

It is a whole new ball game down there among the multi-coloured coral — there were enough fish of all shapes, sizes and colours to start up a sardine factory and that's just within swimming range!

There I was, like some large whale, floating on top of the clear water, trying desperately to keep the snorkel's plastic tubing vertical . . . on the odd occasion I did falter, I almost died of salt poisoning, let alone drown. It's remarkable how a few mouthfuls of sea water can cause a person to lose their composure.

Still, despite my awkward body and primitive swimming technique, there I was being introduced to a world completely foreign to me — a kaleidoscope of living colour just a metre or so below the surface.

I remained entranced by all this activity for almost half an hour until hunger pains got the better of me and the skin on my fingers began to buckle.

Then while I was towelling down, one of my not too terrible bikini clad crew pointed out two blue bottle jelly fish or 'stingers'.

"Now you tell me!" I mentioned.

The reply was: "We didn't see any stingers before you went for a dip!"

Gee, I could have had the three stripes of Adidas etched into my body permanently in the form of a jelly fish scar.

Several beers later I'd forgotten about the incident. We polished off a great nautical lunch . . . and by 4.00 p.m. I was on Hamilton Island —sunburn and all.

I must admit I felt more than a little bit self-conscious walking up the jetty dressed in shorts and thongs and carrying my large black suit case, a suit carrier and brief case!

This evening began at the Bare Foot Bar with the proprietor Wally buying the first cleanser.

The hospitality was sensational and there was a tinge of sadness as I flew out of that man-made paradise for Brisbane.

Tuesday lunch was held in the nostalgic Wisden Room at the Queensland Cricketer's Club. Thirty of Beautyware Baths' top clients were invited to share a few hours at the First Test venue with yours truly providing the laughs.

The Lotus Inn was recommended for the evening meal and was that a spread.

Afterwards we did a couple of laps of honor around the gaming tables at Jupiter's Casino and then parachuted into bed — I'm no big gambler!

Breakfast overlooking the pool was hard to take . . . but I thought bugger it, I really ought to enjoy this scene and I did — croissants and strawberry jam plus a cup of black tea — weak, with a wee wedge of lemon. Beautiful!

12.05 p.m.: I catch the Ansett jet straight through from the Gold Coast to Melbourne.

It was my pleasure to share the company of a 'young' 90-year-old woman who was fascinating to talk to. She was coming home for the 'last time' she told me . . . because her grand-children had voted 4-3 against her to sell the family property — a large acreage in Gippsland!

She'd started from scratch with her husband and now 70 years later, she was finding it difficult to hide her sadness.

Although almost blind, her perspective on life was refreshingly clear . . . "You're never too old to learn! You can be as happy or as miserable as you make it!"

3.15 p.m.: Touch down at Tullamarine and I'm back in town and on the merry-go-round.

4.15 p.m.: Park my car at GTV-9 carpark in Jago St., Richmond.

Now for the rush . . . there is nothing quite like a television newsroom between 5.00 p.m. and six. The hype and energy, first to beat the deadline with a story and secondly to be the best, is great!

The red light on Camera 3 goes on . . . Good evening . . . today . . .!"

The bulletin goes to air on time and without any hiccups.

I've not been home since Saturday morning . . . and it is now Wednesday evening.

The comfort and security of home is precious . . . a home cooked meal at last and a chance to unwind. But only for an hour or two — another yarn has to be written.

I scratch my brains constantly until the nib of my fountain pen is an extension of that grey matter . . . the thoughts begin to make sense on paper and I complete my writing at 1.00 a.m. — I'm tired.

7.00 a.m. it's my first breakfast in a week at home.

9.30 a.m. and I've committed myself to a run in an effort to shed a few pounds that I obviously accumulated on my northern safari. Phew, what a week!

Mixing with the Underworld
'SOME CANDLE, IT WAS A STICK OF DYNAMITE'

It was barely 8 a.m. when the security guard on duty at the Olympic Dam Project site lifted the boom gate to allow the red Falcon entry. My passengers Graham Charlton and Brian Tolhurst were pretty excited at the prospect of exploring the largest uranium ore deposit in the world.

The mere mention of the name Roxby Downs can bring forth an incredibly wide range of reactions from friends and strangers alike. Uranium is a very emotional and political subject — group it with South Africa and religion and you've got the trifecta!

Not many people are given the privilege of a guided tour of the mine — so Graham, Brian and myself jumped at the chance. I might add that the closer we were to actually entering the earth's depths, the more apprehensive we became. In fact it would be fair to say we were quite scared and in Graham's case very frightened! He claimed he was both scared of heights and suffered from claustrophobia — that's no prerequisite for a day in the mines, eh?

Jim Perkins, the man responsible for my visit to the development site, made sure we were well organised and pointed in the right direction — down.

It was a gutsy effort because not only did Jim set up and attend my speaking engagement — he worked night shift right through the early hours and he was still with us when we came out of the mine shaft, four hours later. I like the man's stamina. He'd have made a good medium pacer!

We checked in at the administration block a short distance from the mine shaft. By just reading a few of the signs fixed to the walls of the temporary building, it was easy to see we were in a restricted area: 'Private Property' and 'Trespassers Will Be Prosecuted' notices everywhere. I briefly thought about the potential for my mates and myself becoming radio-active. Uranium has that effect on you! We'd glow at night, eh? No need to turn the lights on at the MCG for night cricket now!

The procedure for checking in was a bit like entering jail, not that I've ever been there!

First we signed a book and handed in our valuables and were told to strip to our underpants. I said to the others, "I hope they are not going to do a body search as well, it could be a bit embarrassing, eh?" They sheepishly agreed trying to quickly camouflage their polar bear white bodies. Three better tans you wouldn't find on three Eskimos!

Dressed in our green all-in-ones and oversize gum boots, we reported to the front desk again. Immediately we were issued with a stack hat complete with battery-operated miner's light — high and low beam too! A very heavy bright blue belt fitted with a battery pack for the floodlight and a safety respirator.

Being naturally inquisitive I asked what it was for. "That's in case something goes wrong down there!" was the reply. "Don't want to get carbon monoxide poisoning, do you?" We all agreed with the simultaneous shake of our heads. Last of all, the bright orange ear-muffs and a brief instruction on how to use the equipment if bad luck and a lot of rock fell on us. Nasty thought, that. The closer we got to the mine shaft and lift, the more prevalent these thoughts became.

Seven of us stood like sardines in yellow raincoats, jammed in a rusty-looking steel bucket. They referred to it as a lift! It hadn't left the surface and it felt very unstable. I looked above me to see several metal ropes disappear over the large guide wheels at the top of the scaffold-like construction tower. The lift was controlled manually from a room some 30 metres away. Here two men are responsible for getting all personnel in and out of the mine as well as getting the copper, gold and uranium ore to the surface.

The ride down was of very poor quality, far inferior to any office block. On the way down it was obvious why we had our raincoats on and our cameras in a plastic bag. Artesian waters spilled down the sides of the crudely cut shaft and onto our colourful helmets. The spillage of water from my stack hat almost drowned the fellas adjacent during the 480 metre journey.

It seemed like eternity getting there and there was no light either — it was impossible for anyone to lift an arm to turn on the floodlights attached to each stack hat.

The steel cable stretched some 1½ metres, I reckon, as we pulled up short of our exit level in the pitch-black, hot mine shaft — we began to bob up and down like a yo-yo. Frightening stuff. Several expletives were uttered to relieve the nervous tension.

We filed out of the lift like the seven dwarfs strolling after Snow White, Indian file. Now for the action.

To my amazement it was just like a mini township carved out of the earth, between 300 and 500 metres below the ground. It was mentioned that the mineral deposits present extend to some 26 square miles or the size of a city like Adelaide. Mining was being carried out on three levels within the rich deposit range.

The speed limit along any tunnel was 8 kmh — forwards or backwards. Some of the vehicular machinery underground was enormous — 50 tonne pickup trucks with wheels the size of a man and with flashing blue lights were a common sight.

Most of the larger tunnel walls and ceilings had been sprayed white to reflect the light from fluorescent fixtures which disappeared into tiny white spots along the direction of each excavation. Everywhere safety signs confronted us as a sure indication of the serious and dangerous mode of operations carried out. The movement of air fascinated me. Large canvas fan-driven socks were slung from wall fixtures along with the power and water tubing. It was possible to move the air from its intake position to 600 metres into each level.

The relative levels of each shaft were clearly marked on the rock face in large bold black numbers. Each level had been accurately plotted with the use of a laser beam.

Three hours below ground seemed like half an hour, I couldn't get enough of the place. The weight of my emergency power pack and safety respirator became almost non-existent as I continually aimed my camera at a new and different aspect of the mining process.

There were about 300 personnel on the site working 24 hours around the clock.

We travelled the length and breadth of the developed mine in a filthy white jeep, sending out a wake of mud. It was like being in the movie 'Indiana Jones and The Temple of Doom'. You drive around almost oblivious to what's happening just around the corner, because of the continual sound of the mine. Every now and then a 50 tonne loader approached and it would threaten and intimidate the uninitiated in such a confined space — which was just the width of the pick-up trucks in many cases.

On the way to a drilling site, I sat on something on the car seat. It felt like a candle. Some candle, it was a stick of gelignite without the detonator! My heartbeat increased twofold especially as I was not to take photographs of the explosive stores because the heat of the flashlight might send up the entire area in smoke. Needless to say I was very careful where I aimed my camera.

The driller is a skilled man. We talked to Steve and his understudy, or apprentice, Joe. Once an ore deposit is established, the driller prepares the drive face for the powder monkey to come in and set the explosives. The skill of these men is evident when watching the precision used to position about 70 holes to accept the sticks of gelignite.

Apparently the technique is to plan the drilling chart in parallel lines and diagonals, with a couple of extra sticks in the middle so that the fractures focus towards the middle of the explosion, bringing the rock face down. The machinery used to make these holes is a bit like a multi-armed dentist's drill, on wheels. My teeth ached just looking at it.

Then the powder monkeys come in behind the drillers, clear the area, and set the explosives in position. A count-down and then 'Boooooomm!'. Even though we were some 70 metres from the blasting, the vibration was unreal in the ribcage. So too was the sound and movement of air.

Now I know what it must feel like to be a fish in the river when some crazy person decides to use dynamite instead of a bent nail.

Generally an explosion of that dimension will increase the tunnel or shaft by removing 400 tonnes of rock. That is in volume six metres wide, about 4.5 metres high and up to 3.8 metres in depth. Some blast, eh?

Then along come the team of extractors and their heavy mobilised machinery to transport the rock to an area called the open hole. With the use of a large vibrating machine, the ore is collected ready to relay to daylight. The capacity of each bucket lifted to the surface is about six tonnes, and the trip up takes on average 100 seconds.

In all a fascinating and eye-opening experience. Time was against us as we had to be in other parts of South Australia that night. But we couldn't leave without eating at the 'Hard Rock Cafe', also underground.

A cup of coffee took the dusty coating from my tongue and I could bring myself to tackle the meat pies from the micro-wave oven.

I'd taken my hard hat off to drink, placed it on the table and forgotten about it. On the word "go" I immediately jumped to my feet ready to catch our ride upstairs, forgot about my helmet, which was attached to my battery pack, comfortably supported by my buttocks. The result was a runaway helmet on the table top and tangled lead around my feet. Sugar, sauce and tupperware containers, followed me to the floor. It is a good thing I'm not a miner.

Recruit for the fight against evil

'*I RAISED MY HAND ABOVE MY HEAD AND READ THE SACRED OATH*'

Life's journey is so full of unexpected meetings. But in my wildest dreams I never expected to come face to face with that famous comic book hero — The Phantom! I had just sat down after about an hour on my feet entertaining a wonderfully receptive audience at the Western District Aussie Rules Football Club in Brisbane.

It was a hot, sticky night and the beads of perspiration were pouring forth from my forehead at an embarrassing rate and forming rivulets of good honest sweat down the both sides of my face.

Showing a lot of class, I wiped my leaking brow and glowing cheeks with the bright red paper napkin I hadn't used after my main course.

Sitting on the top table at any function can be a bit like 'spotlight on sport' with about 200 plus sets of beady eyes dwelling on your every movement... in fact it's very difficult to pick your teeth in private if the steak has been too tough, or if the gap between your front teeth is now clogged with a delightful piece of golden corn so elegantly gnashed off the cob earlier in the night.

Nevertheless the idea is to appear unruffled by all the attention and act naturally, which is exactly what I was doing... just chatting away with the club president and signing a few autographs.

Then — I saw this strange character making his way to the official table. I couldn't believe my eyes!

The humidity was stickier than a desert drover's armpits and here's a guy dressed in a full length overcoat, cravat, sunglasses and top hat.

It was a capacity crowd. Yes, they were hanging from the rafters that night and as the masses made their way to the public conveniences in the foyer during a break, this joker forced his way against the traffic flow, to the front of the entertainment room, where we were seated.

At that time I said to the president, "'Ave a go at this bloke — I bet he wants to get in my ear!"

I couldn't help but add, "I bet he's a live one, this fella!"

He arrived, as large as life, in front of the decorated trestle and introduced himself: "Mr Walker . . . the ghost who walks."

I thought to myself, "Oh, oh, I wasn't wrong — he reckons he's the Phantom."

It was very difficult to prevent myself from laughing — a sly grin crept out from under my moustache!

He thrust his hand towards me in a positive manner of greeting and said, "From one Mr Walker to another, it's an honour to meet you!" Needless to say his hand was very clammy, but a vice-like grip accompanied the dampness.

My thoughts were: "He's fair dinkum, this bloke."

Then he started peeling off his clothes, item by item.

Off came the cravat, sun glasses and hat. Sure enough he had the distinctive eye pieces to conceal his identity.

As he took off his overcoat, he revealed the skin-tight, grey body suit with the diagonal, black-striped jocks.

His belt supported some sorts of firearms and the famous skull sign covered his navel.

Yes it was him — the ghost who walks.

But why me? How was I going to explain this fellow at question time, soon to follow.

He wasn't shy either. He quickly called for two glasses of milk so I could take the sacred oath — to serve the world, against evil.

Now milk's not one of my favourite drinks, but I thought any minute now I'll be hearing the beat of jungle drums in the distance saying, "Drink the milk Tangles or you're dead!'' Or maybe dozens of pygmies would come rushing at me through the club rooms.

The other coincidence was . . . the phantom's girlfriend is named Diana. Well, so too was the young woman waiting on our table that evening.

So what could I do? I raised my right hand above my head and read 'the sacred oath'.

"I promise to fight on the side of the weak against the oppressor with good against evil, and to do everything in my power to destroy greed, cruelty and injustice wherever it exists . . . and may my children follow after me."

My friend and Channel 9 cricket commentator Bill Lawry was nicknamed 'The Phantom' because he always had a Phantom comic in his back pocket during his playing days.

As I later discovered, Bill was a member of the Phantom Club of Australia.

Today there are over 3500 members of the club — they share good times and a large range of recreational activities.

In my case I was proud to accept a life membership of the club and it really is quite amazing just where and when you run into Phantom "phriends".

For the uninitiated: some 400 years ago the lone survivor of a pirate raid was washed up on a remote Bengali beach. On the skull of his father's murderer he swore an oath to fight crime. Generations followed him. The pygmy Bandar people believed it was always the same man. "The ghost who walks," they said. So the legend grew. A name whispered, loved, and feared . . . The Phantom.

He's pretty good — The Phantom.

But I wonder how well he'd cope batting against the four-pronged pace attack of the West Indies. Maybe they'd respect him too much to get him out?

It's amazing how a perfectly normal beginning to a fun night can be turned into a deadly serious commitment to fight evil at all times . . . all it took was a couple of milks, eh?

I repeat, "Long live the ghost who walks — and that applies to Bill Lawry, too!"

The Quick and the Hungry

'AS HUNGRY AS I WAS, SOMEHOW THE OFFERING LACKED QUITE A DEAL OF APPEAL'

Apart from the fundraising side of many public speaking engagements, which is always near the top of the priority list, there is always the menu to struggle through before being given control of the microphone.

Now, some nights are better organised than others. This is generally reflected in the choice of food — a quick and easy solution is often the good old chook!

Yes, in the industry the nightly vigil is called the 'chicken circuit'. How do you feel about eating chicken (hot or cold, it doesn't really matter) on average nine out of every 10 nights on the road?

Well, I'm not a huge wrap for chicken. In fact, I haven't been since my three-month-long diet of rubberised waterfowl in the West Indies, way back in 1973. Gee, they were tough old birds!

Just the thought of eating chook these days is fairly unpalatable even with a bottle or two of champagne. Not that I get to sip that too often at a sports night.

Although once recently, while on a working adventure to North Queensland, I was lucky enough to sink one or two glasses of the good stuff, but that was before heading off to the venue for our little chat . . . I should have known it was too good to be true when the receptionist handed me the key to room No. 13 — "The one with a great view," she stated.

Sure enough, the night rolled on through a comedy of errors . . . and I must confess if Australia is going to show off to the world what a marvellous country we live in, then our attitude to serving tourists definitely needs a kick in the pants. After all, first impressions are lasting.

I knew we were operating on Queensland time and were looking to an 8 p.m. 'sit down' for the meal, but ten minutes past nine is running a bit behind schedule even in that sort of balmy night air, especially when the caterer wants to finish by 10 p.m. with a view to avoiding paying his indifferent staff for an extra hour's toil. A 10 o'clock finish on Saturday night anywhere in the world is optimistic! And the way this crew were travelling, there was no hope!

The eating format for the evening was Coles cafeteria-style for the entree and smorgasbord for the main course. Now, I don't mind queuing up for a meal . . . I've been doing that all my life, but the invited guests' table was the last one to join what turned out to be a long and restless line of hungry people.

Before any of our table members got near the hot lamps shining on the servery area, the word was out — there was no beef stroganoff left! We must have been standing patiently for almost 15 minutes before that bad news.

Wait for the excuse . . . "Gee, they never usually eat an entree, so we didn't make much!" said the empty-handed chef.

Nevertheless, there just happened to be plenty of rice . . . but let's be honest, plain white rice tastes pretty awful on its own without some sort of gravy or sauce to cover its bland, clag-like nature. Even the gravy leftovers were gone!

So an alternative was offered — one very skinny slice of ham topped with a circular piece of pineapple. By the time this appetising little number was offered, the rice bed was stone motherless cold.

As hungry as I was, somehow the offering lacked quite a deal of appeal. I thought to myself, it can only get better from here on in. I just kept on grinning and pressed on down the line.

Again we were last to fill our plates with the remnants of what must have been a great spread . . . I knocked over three blokes getting to the last half a dozen prawns. All the chicken breasts and drumsticks had been sifted through and only the bones remained.

By now I was getting a little nervous before my talk and I lost my appetite.

Meanwhile, the quick and the hungry locals managed to keep downing the odd glass or dozen of cold beer . . . they had loosened up considerably from the quiet group of people that started the evening.

Yes, the time was ripe to launch into a few stories to entertain the gathering because a belly full of food and plenty of liquid refreshments had certainly put the crowd in the right frame of mind.

Their response was fantastic but my task was made all the more difficult by the heavy-handed waitresses collecting the plates as I spoke . . . the amplification of the cups, saucers and plates was very, very high in the shiny-surfaced room.

Forty-five minutes later I had finished . . . so too had the eager catering staff who were very keen to be off the premises. Several people moved to the back of the room in search of some sweets, but they had disappeared into thin air.

This time the explanation was . . . "No one seemed to want any, so we took them away thinking we could use them at tomorrow night's function."

After some very stern words to the head caterer, the apple slices and cream reappeared!

Now our only problem was . . . how we were going to eat them? The rubbish removers had been instructed to pick up the dessert spoons as well . . . and they did!

At the top table I ate my sweets with the tiny spoon out of the sugar bowl. When I had finished scraping the bottom of my bowl, I handed it on to the other patient gentleman sitting next to me.

At this stage the thought of a nice coffee and port took my fancy.

You are not going to believe this . . . they ran out of hot water for the tea and coffee. Gee, I'm glad there were only 125 people present — imagine the problems 250 people would have created?

One young lady, who was lucky enough to have her cup filled with coffee, then suffered the disappointment of seeing it whisked away from under her nose before she could finish it!

A couple of beers later and chat with all and sundry brought the night to a satisfactory end, or so I thought.

It was 1.30, Sunday morning and my room key — No. 13 — was still at reception. This was shaping up as a major problem because the lobby area of the plush hotel was dark and deserted.

I remembered looking out of my window earlier in the night and thinking, what a magnificent view across the ocean, so I didn't lock the sliding doors because my room was on the second floor.

Now try to visualise a 17-stone man, with several drinks under the belt, attempting to scale the well-balconied facade of the building.

I was within metres of my destination when a security guard appeared and scared the living daylights out of me. He also had a companion who was breathing very heavily — a German shepherd watchdog!

It all ended on a tired, yet happy note, when the guard shoved me over the balcony of No. 13 with both hands. Perhaps I would wake up with a start to find the night was only a dream, but no such luck.

I hoped I don't get too many more night like that one, I'd even prefer a three-course chicken meal, and I mean it!

The Great Kiwi Debate

'NEW ZEALAND IS A PLACE WHERE MEN ARE DUBIOUS AND SHEEP ARE SLOW'

How does the idea of travelling to Wellington, NZ, for a live radio debate on the subject of 'Kiwis Do It Better' sound? I was a bit apprehensive at first, until the organisers of the event mentioned I would be captain of a three-man team, including Tony Greig, the former England cricket captain, and Australian rugby union champion Roger Gould.

But the most attractive aspect of the trip was that our team would debate the negative side of the argument, which I must admit did sit rather comfortably with all three of us!

Our opponents were, as it turned out, three well-rehearsed and talented orators on the topic. A learned man named Jim Hopkins was leader of the opposition and unfortunately he was brilliant . . .

Batting No. 2 for NZ was a batsman used to the position — John Reid who's main claim to fame is being a cousin of ultra tall Test bowler Bruce Reid.

Third, was a grim, determined All Black named Andy Hayden who definitely looked over-dressed in a dinner suit — the attire mentioned on the invitation.

Obviously, Kiwis don't take any notice because Jim Hopkins was clad in anything but a 'dickie-bird' suit. His white crumpled cotton jacket and light brown shirt would have looked more at home on a university campus . . . and from the length of his greying hair and manner of speaking, he had obviously spent many a year doing just that — maybe even decades!

Each speaker was given six minutes to verbally assault the subject through a microphone which carried our verbal joust to 32 radio stations around NZ — I thought they only had two and that they went off air at 9 p.m.!

After five minutes, a huge gong was belted . . . the loud message being simply — one minute to wrap up!

Tony Greig so correctly quipped, "Five minutes is ample time to present the positive side of 'Kiwis do it better' but six minutes is not nearly enough time to tear the statement apart"!

After the crowd of 500 (497 Kiwis) stopped booing, the big blond all-rounder continued . . . "We'd need about 45 minutes each!"

So as you can so clearly see, the visiting group were on a hiding to nothing in front of a very parochial home crowd.

Our 'three wise men' had been given absolutely no chance to recover from a torrid Air New Zealand landing (the pilot must have been a taxi-driver in his spare time) into a stiff breeze on the extremely short runway at Wellington Airport.

Anyhow, we decided not to go down without giving 'em heaps! And we did.

On the stroke of 8 p.m. Kiwi-time, the exaggerated Kiwi voice of the master of ceremonies stated unashamedly, that he'd tossed the coin and Australia would speak first.

It was a lie, and I didn't want all of those New Zealanders who had tuned into their crystal sets for the night's entertainment to think we were wimps, so I jumped to the lectern and set the story straight. I took a 'two bob' bit out of my trouser pocket, tossed it high in the air, where it sparkled like a jewel in the night against the bright television spotlights. I grabbed it as only a great fine leg fieldsman could and shouted, "Heads or tails?"

Before I got even a semblance of an answer from the local boys, who by the way couldn't believe their eyes, I put the 20 cent piece back where it belonged in the pocket of my hired dinner suit and quietly said, "Bad luck fellas, we win — you talk first!"

By the time my tail hit the seat, 10-15 seconds of pregnant silence had elapsed, and believe me that's a lot of silence on radio.

So we caught 'em with their pants down, but I must admit, some six minutes later, we almost wished we hadn't pulled our brazen stunt.

The eccentric Jim Hopkins landed some very low body blows which even hurt Tony Greig, who has finally come to his senses after leaving South Africa and England, and settling in Australia.

It's common knowlege that the demographic centre of NZ is right plonk in the middle of Bondi Junction, a mere Aussie place-kick away from the Sydney Cricket Ground.

While thousands of Kiwis are on the dole in our country and I don't think they should be allowed to get away with it . . . only 37 Australian born persons, from whom I wish to dissociate myself, are registered on the dole in NZ. I can't understand them because even with the drop in the Aussie dollar they're still getting paid less.

Needless to say, dingoes, beer, cricket and the Olympic Games were heavily commented on by the home side!

So I bit the bullet and went for broke. I doubt if New Zealand radio will ever be the same again . . . and not purely because of our strine and Afrikaans accents.

"Australia is a country where men are men and sheep are nervous . . . on the other hand, New Zealand is a place where men are dubious and sheep are slow . . . and the sale of gumboots very high — not necessarily to stop tinea," I said.

More boos, but I continued.

"What about your Prime Minister? At least our PM can handle the Pritikin diet. The best your bloke can do is go on a 'staple diet'! (The Kiwi PM has had his stomach stapled if you didn't happen to know). And wait until the rust sets in — he'll go real ordinary then!"

They didn't like it!

"How about 'Piggy' Muldoon (no offence) but didn't he over-react a bit after the under-arm incident? He practically wanted to declare war on Australia and now big American boats aren't allowed to park in Wellington Harbor. Whatever happened to the ANZUS pact?"

Deathly silence greeted that one!

When Tony Greig asked the women to take a long hard look at the fellas sitting next to them or opposite, more shouts of contempt.

"There must be some doubt about him, droopy moustache, longish hair and sideburns, pale face, pot belly, poor conversationalist . . . does he really do it better? If there isn't a doubt, then you haven't tried the real thing!"

That one went down like a lead balloon, but I liked it!

Roger Gould gave 'em plenty on the rugby union scene where coach Alan Jones and Australia is dominating the world.

"I haven't forgotten about the K-27 or 'plastic fantastic'," I said.

Unfortunately, it took a Belgian-born, Australian businessman to have the foresight to enter a challenge for the America's Cup on behalf of the Kiwis.

Do they do it better?

Nice of the Kiwis to take their plastic toy boat out of the bath and finally give it a go in some real water off Fremantle.

There's nothing to write home about in NZ either . . . they spat the dummy when a core sample from their yacht was mentioned. That story hardly made a ripple in Australian waters but was front page for three days in NZ and even then the papers were a day late.

The pilot of the plane said, "Turn our watches on two hours when we arrive." I reckon the clock should be turned back 10 years.

Sorry if I've offended any Kiwis, but it was a great debate . . . I'll admit we lost, but not by much.

Also I should mention the new DB Kiwi Lager — the reason for our gathering was to launch this new export lager. It's not a bad drop. I especially like the label colours, Australian green and gold.

C'mon Aussie C'mon!

New Zealand is a place where men are dubious and sheep are slow . . .

Chapter Five

AMUSING MOMENTS ON TOUR

. . . built for midgets, I kept walking into rafters.

From a hotel somewhere . . .

'I REALLY OBJECTED TO THE ANTS WHICH MARCHED FROM THE POWERPOINTS'

I'm writing this in a hotel room in Canberra, Sydney or Adelaide. At this time of the season, there's not too much point caring where you are, so long as you are in the right place for the right game of cricket.

Actually, booking into and out of hotels has been very much part of my life since I started in first class cricket.

I guess it all began on my first trip, to the Caribbean in 1973. The 38-hour flight wasn't much fun because I had the misfortune to be sitting between Doug Walters and Terry Jenner, who both took turns spilling beer on my lap and blowing smoke over me.

I was relieved to reach Kingston, Jamaica, and particularly delighted that I was not to be the brunt of a practical joke which lasted the whole tour.

We stayed at the Courtley Manor Hotel, which comprised of a series of bungalows surrounding a pool.

The local brew was Red Stripe, which we grew to regard highly. So popular was it in fact, that a barrel was organised to be stationed outside Room 14, the abode of Walters and Jenner.

I figured I could get used to that style of life, especially when the Appleton Rum Co. supplied all the blokes with bottles of rum and whisky, and cigarettes came gratis too.

Certainly some of the boys declared they were in paradise, being in the Caribbean, ogling the bikini-clad beauties, enjoying free rum and puffing on a fag. Too bad we had to play cricket!

Naturally, all this wasn't enough for Doug Walters, who simply couldn't stop himself from organising a practical joke. The target was that Newcastle leggie, Johnny 'Whokka' Watkins, a real country boy at heart. Now Doug and Whokka became great mates during the third Test against Pakistan at the SCG just a few weeks earlier.

Now this was the first time that Whokka had travelled out of Australia, and someone had spooked him about all the black power movement in the West Indies.

Dougie thought he would take advantage of it, and when he was asked for advice, he instructed Whokka to make peace offerings each night. So at two o'clock one morning, Whokka left two packets of cigs outside his room on the 'Welcome' mat, and to his delight, they were gone when he woke up.

This went on for several days, and then Doug suggested his new mates might be looking for something different. The rum went out the next night, the scotch the next, more fags, and on and on throughout the next couple of months.

Eventually, a couple of the boys informed Whokka that the 'mates' were

Walters and Jenner. He didn't believe it, and I don't think he does to this day.

Hotels around the world are not all top class, and, having survived several unsavory incidents, it is fun to reflect on some of the experiences. Actually the Australians moved out of only one hotel during my career. That was a hotel in Auckland, New Zealand.

I remember booking into the room, and spending 20 minutes squashing giant mosquitos on the ceiling by hurling my cricket boots. Now I have reasonably big boots, and I was killing them by the dozen, but still I reckon I hadn't nailed half the population before I retreated to the bar.

That's when we were harrassed by lady bowlers from Queensland, who arrived by bus and immediately became excited and enthralled to meet the Aussie players. It was a long way from the bikini girls of Kingston, I can tell you.

Next morning, after the mosquitos had taken revenge for my attempted annihilation the previous night, I headed off to complain to our skipper Ian Chappell. But he was already in the foyer, checking out!

There's a hotel in Georgetown, Guyana, which isn't my kind of place either.

I decided to shower when I arrived in my room, which obviously hadn't been used for a couple of years. The water came gushing from the shower, and I stepped into the metre square cubicle. Suddenly three monstrous cockroaches bounded from the shower plug, and for a bloke my size, there just wasn't room for four of us!

The lizards on the ceiling caused only minor concern after that, but I really objected to the ants which marched from the powerpoints. Whenever you changed your clothes, you had to check, and inevitably, remove an ant nest.

The food wasn't for a connoisseur either, although there were 25 varieties of curried goat. At one stage, Dougie Walters decided to have a steak, but even with the sharp knife, he couldn't cut it, let alone eat it. He asked for something softer, and eventually settled for tomato soup.

I thoroughly enjoyed my journeys to England, but even there a few problems can arise.

The Dolphin is a grand old pub in Somerset and a genuine part of the history of the area. The only problem was that it must have been built for midgets, because I kept walking into rafters. Fair dinkum, Bruce 'Stumpy' Laird ducked when he walked through a doorway!

Even the grand Waldorf in London had a drawback. I guess we were unlucky in 1975 that England endured a heat wave — there is no air conditioning at The Waldorf. The meeting place for breakfast was in the corridor, where the players sat in a huddle, enjoying the air which occasionally found its way through the emergency exit door.

Parking around The Waldorf can be dicey too. I remember having a match off, and Ian Chappell and Rod Marsh decided we should spend it in

London. We had three Jaguars at our disposal — a red one, a blue one and a yellow one, just so we each knew which car was our own.

We gave the commissionaire a fist full of coins to 'feed' the meters during the appropriate hours, and settled in for a good night. Imagine my horror when, next morning, I looked out the window to discover that the red and blue Jags weren't there. I figured it would take a lot of explaining to the company which lent us the expensive wheels.

I rang all over London before I was told that the cars weren't stolen, but had been towed away and impounded! I didn't know until then that feeding the meter was equally as bad as not putting any money in at all, and that they actually towed the offending cars away.

Now we had a golf game organised for 11.00 a.m. and what was to be a relaxing day, with no expense, turned into a nightmare. I reckoned I handed over £100 before I reached the course. It cost me 33 quid to regain possession of EACH car, plus taxi fares, phone calls and a meal on the run.

To make matters worse Chappell and Bacchus (Rod Marsh) insisted the fines be settled on the golf course. As a golfer, I am a good pace bowler. I swing the ball both ways in the air. In fact, the only bonus came at the 13th, when an inswinger went so far into the rough that I found six balls on the way out.

At Leeds (UK) we stayed at a marvellous hotel, surrounded by countryside riddled with rabbits. These little bunnies would sit on the lawns of the hotel, as placidly as you like, until someone attempted to touch them.

One night, after a team meeting, a group of players decided to find a torch and go rabbit hunting, but alas, the rabbits, particularly in the early hours of the morning, were far too elusive.

There was considerable noise apparently, and most of the hotel guests were witnesses to the hunt. Team manager, Fred Bennett, heard of it and next morning he went to make an official apology to the manager. He was given a warm welcome, told not to give it another thought and that it was all good, healthy fun.

Fred couldn't believe the generous response, and it wasn't until some time later that we told him the manager was one of the posse!

Actually I should have known all about pub life and the sort of things which go on. My dad, 'Big Max', ran the Empire hotel in Hobart and I still have vivid memories of those days.

I remember studying for my mid-year exams and feeling happy that I had physics totally covered for the next day. I was set to slay 'em.

Unfortunately, there was a big Test in England at the time, and Big Max decided to have over a lot of his mates, who also happened to be his customers, for a few 'friendlies' and a listen to the radio.

The licensing board heard about the function, which naturally was 'after hours' and decided to raid the place. But my old man heard they were on the way, and told everyone to get into my room, because that was sacrosanct as far as the licensing boys were concerned.

There I was, rudely awakened by two giants slumping on the end of my bed, spilling beer on my sheets. In the corner was another bloke whose intentions were clear — he had a lass on his knee, and I am certain his mind wasn't on the glass of beer in his free hand. There were blokes in every corner, laughing and yelling, fully aware that the licensing boys were outside the door, unable to enter.

I somehow passed the exam.

On another occasion a pleasant Sunday morning for the locals was in jeopardy because the booze had run out, so everyone adjourned to the Empire. There were more cars parked in front of the pub than outside the church, a little way down the street, and perhaps that was why the licensing boys became suspicious. Anyway, this time there was no warning, until the car arrived.

We were having renovations done at the time, and Big Max told everyone to get out the back and start unloading the bricks from a truck.

'Inkie' Anning, who was a bricklaying contractor, took charge, and everyone looked feverishly busy when the raid was made. The only trouble was that most of the blokes had enjoyed a few too many beers, and they surrounded the truck with a neat stack of bricks.

The raiders couldn't find my dad, who was hiding under a boat in the backyard. The licensing boys had to accept Inkie's explanation that the work had to be done in a hurry, and another disaster was averted.

Anyway, another day, another pub . . .

A One-Day Wonder

'IT WAS ONE OF THE GREAT MOMENTS IN MY CAREER'

One-day cricket has grown into a great spectacle with world championships played around the globe. Those Australians who witnessed the World Championship played in Melbourne and Sydney in 1985 will certainly agree. What a marvellous success it was.

Ultimately, the final on March 10, at the MCG, was contested between two traditional rivals, India and Pakistan.

It really was quite an odd occasion in sport. There we had 10 Muslims and one Hindu wearing the colours of Pakistan, playing in a game of cricket against an Indian team consisting of 10 Hindus and one Muslim, to help celebrate the 150th birthday of an antipodean state — Victoria.

The Indian eight wicket victory gave them a handsome trophy to place alongside their World Cup of '83 at Lord's and the Asia Cup, won the previous year. To boot, they collected 288,000 rupees ($32,000) for their few weeks in Australia. No doubt they enjoyed the western life style along the way.

So in the end, four years of expert planning and endeavour by the organisers were rewarded with a profit believed to be almost $1 million.

I was lucky enough to play in the inaugural World Cup final against the West Indies at Lords in 1975. That game was one of the greatest one-day games played. I couldn't believe the transition in the crowds at Lord's for a West Indies v Australia contest.

When playing England, most of the spectators, particularly in the Members, had grey striped, three-piece suits on and none of them were in any danger of getting bruised hands from over-clapping. Yet, for that memorable final, the crowd had began to swell into the confines of the ground well before 9 o'clock in the morning.

The guys dressed in green coats with the MCG logo on their pockets, control the flow of people with the action of a footpedal. The turnstiles were jammed chock full at 9.15 a.m. and seeing the enormous queues almost 800 yards long and as many as five deep, several of the gate keepers decided not to clip a hole in the entrance tickets in order to get the masses inside before the first ball was bowled at 10 a.m.

Ninety per cent of the crowd were West Indians who had arrived to see their brothers beat the living daylights out of the Australians.

Some of the more enterprising spectators realised their tickets hadn't been cancelled, and not averse to helping a friend in need of a ticket, came up with the idea of placing their ticket inside a quickly emptied beer can. Next the can was heaved over the wall. The strongest competitors for the can generally won out and immediately gained entrance to the ground.

Needless to say, by 10.30 a.m. the West Indian supporters were everywhere and anywhere they could put their backsides down. And they are wonderfully active crowds to play in front of!

The West Indies batted first and my role in the field was to sweep around the boundary line, from fine-leg to deep mid-wicket. Can you imagine a guy of lesser pace and ability than yours truly managing to cope? It gave me a beaut opportunity to communicate with the people just outside the ropes.

'Colourful' is not the only word to describe them. Noisy yes! They were banging sticks against rubbish bins, knocking bottles together and I'll never forget one huge mountain of a man, with muscles growing out of muscles, brandishing a very large brass bell above his head.

The sound was a haunting, pulsating rhythm, a bit like a heart beat but very much aligned to reggae music, I'm told. Can you imagine a guy conducting a primitive orchestra with a bell in one hand and a bottle of rum in the other. Well, that was exactly it.

Then there was the boundary rider or cheerleader. She was a magnificent young woman about 21, poured into a nipple pink singlet with no bra. I only realised that condition as she swayed from side to side like a pendulum in perfect timing with the big fella.

Whilst all this was going on, so too was the game. Not an easy position to field, square leg, eh?

The crowd remained involved in proceedings in the middle for the entire game, waiting for the last Australian wicket to fall. That was Jeff Thomson, batting at No. 11, caught at mid-off. Except it was a no-ball!

In failing light it took almost eight minutes to get the grassed area free from rejoicing fans. Finally the last wicket stand between Dennis Lillee and Jeff Thomson was broken and victory went the way of the West Indies by 16 runs.

Some three hours later on, darkness hung over the home of cricket. From the players balcony we could see and hear more than 10,000 ecstatic West Indies supporters chanting and singing their calypso songs. It was one of the great moments in my career as a sportsman. Despite our loss on that day, the game of cricket had won and won well.

From that game we have seen many changes to the one-day international. A dramatic series of events led to the World Series Cricket revolution in 1977, with magnate Kerry Packer being the architect.

He made it happen, and a game called 'pyjama cricket under lights' by the English press, has evolved into an established form of the game.

Trials of the Typewriter
'IT WOULD BE FAIR TO SAY THIS FELLOW WASN'T YOUR AVERAGE INDIAN MAHARAJAH'

While most of the publicity about the game of cricket is the responsibility of journalists and commentators, the average cricket follower knows little about how tough it can be getting the story of a day's play to air or into print.

Almost 40 members of the 'poisoned typewriters club' followed the 1986-87 clashes for the Ashes contest around Australia.

These print gurus sometimes go to extraordinary lengths to make sure their impressions of a day's play are filed on time.

It's generally not a problem in Australia and England, but a very different story in places like India and Pakistan.

For instance during Australia's official tour of India, Mike Coward of the *Sydney Morning Herald* ran into a few problems. The team was playing its second tour match at a town called Gwalior which, by the way, had never before hosted an international cricket match, let alone provide a facility for an international press corps.

The locals constructed a large tent and provided two telex machines and two operators — neither men nor machines worked!

Then an impassioned plea was made to the Maharajah of Gwalior, who was educated at Oxford and wore a yellow Lacoste shirt. It would be fair to say this fellow wasn't your average Indian maharajah.

The seven-man contingent was the largest press corps sent by the Australian media to India . . . and the group was getting a bit edgy.

The game finished at 4.30 p.m. (with a 4½ hour time difference that was 9.00 p.m. Sydney time).

The Maharajah didn't let Mike and his fellow journalists down — he supplied a car plus a driver. Mike was rushed from the ground to a textile mill some 11 km away, and with him was copy from everyone else.

So the first day's copy was sent via a textile factory, nowhere near the playing ground . . . the people of India proved to be very generous on this occasion. The owner had gone to school with Mike and subsequently sent his own telex operators back to the primitive tent at the ground to look after the press!

The 'Magic 7' moved on to Rojkot for the fourth and final one day international — this is the city where Mahatma Gandhi was born and educated.

There was no telex at all, which proved to be most distressing to all of the correspondents.Still the game's not over until the last ball is bowled.

The collective creative talents of the corps soon discovered several bizarre spots to file their copy from — one from a diesel engine company, another from a hotel, the post office was worth a try and Alan Shiell from Adelaide finally got his copy sorted out and sent from a steel tubing company!

Today's journalists rely heavily on modern technology to file their stories and all of the new devices are dependent on a sophisticated phone system — India was definitely not offering that facility!

'Type-Corder' is the name of the mini-computer that most journalists use — it consists of a typewriter keyboard plus a screen. The difficulty is that the writer can only have seven lines of text on the screen at once. More difficult for the thought process than having a whole sheet in front of them.

The overwhelming plus for the system is the advantage of time saved. This is especially beneficial in day/night games — there's no time wasted dictating copy.

The 'coupler' is fitted over the phone receiver like a pair of galoshes over a shoe. A command is struck into the typewriter and into the system — the story and copy passes rapidly down the line out into the office computer.

This system only works in Australia, England, South Africa and New Zealand. India, Pakistan, Sri Lanka and the West Indies are hopeless places even to make a simple phone call!

Phil Wilkins of *The Australian* tells me even the technology can go wrong if you're not careful . . . and it did!

While covering the rebel tour of South Africa at Bloemfontein, the birthplace of former Australian opener Keppler Wessels, he ran into trouble.

'Filthy Phil' as he is affectionately known to his mates, had to file three stories back to Sydney, Australia. It was 8.00 p.m. South African time and about 10 minutes of computer time was all that was required to span the ocean.

the cricket copy is coming through from the press corps now...

Snake Charmer Soap

And speaking of the wonderful invention — a telephone — it proved to be quite the centre of controversy at Lord's in 1972.

He rang head office in Sydney to check if they'd received his stories — no story had arrived!

So every 25 minutes, for three hours, Phil sent his copy to Australia at a cost of $56 a call. After eight calls the cost for failure was $448.

Where the exercise had broken down was that the new computer system wouldn't marry into the old fashioned switchboard employed by his place of abode! In the end he walked to the cricket ground where he frightened the living daylights out of a black armed guard who was fast asleep near the entrance, under a pine tree.

Finally he convinced the guard to let him into the press box. By this time it was well after midnight and there was no electricity in the box . . . so there he was with this big black man holding a torch over his shoulder while he worked. And the paper went to print on time.

Phil Wilkins used to write for the *Sydney Morning Herald* before joining *The Australian*. And on his very first day, the new boy made an unforgiveable 'blue'.

His problem was the phone numbers — *SMH* 20944 and *The Australian* 20925. Phil rang through his very first article to what he thought was *The Australian*, but instead he'd filed with his former employer — the *SMH*.

Two hours later the editor of the SMH rang *The Australian* to ask if they wanted Phil Wilkins 'because he's filed it with us!'

Another problem arose when Sydney-based cricket writer Dick Tucker suggested a phone was necessary at a ground to file through running copy. The blunt answer was simply, "No way!"

Isn't it amazing that if you happen to know someone with influence you can achieve almost anything. Former England captain and aristocrat 'Lord' Ted Dexter had managed to bring his own portable TV to the ground on Saturday afternoon to watch the races. Dick's immediate reaction after feeling cheated was to speak to the people in power, again pointing out the imbalance.

No problems, Dick had his phone and Lord Ted got to watch his races.

Then there was the AAP representative at Faisalabad in 1984, Ross Mullins. Ross set out in a motorised tricycle to file an urgent despatch from the second Test match between Pakistan and Australia.

The engine in the auto-rickshaw had less guts than a lawn mower. The road to the telegraph station was strewn with potholes and the tricycle discovered a new one — at some pace too!

The rickshaw rolled over at quite a fair pace . . . Ross reckoned a steel girder on the side of the road ripped through the machine like a can opener, just missing him.

The copy just had to be filed, so Ross used the metal girder as a lever, to right the fallen rickshaw! Copy was successfully filed, despite the team doctor Paul Kronig back at the ground pronouncing mild shock and abrasions. After an aspirin and a nap, Ross was back on deck later.

Apparently it is always advisable to carry lots of cigarettes and coins of the realm if you want to avoid lengthy delays . . . but a need for diplomacy is essential.

The other consideration too is that Moslems pray five times a day. It is not unusual to witness two telex operators sitting cross-legged, holding hands in prayer for 45 minutes or more, depending on their mood at the time.

So next time you sit down to breakfast with coffee, toast, and a broadsheet newspaper, take a minute to appreciate how difficult it may have been to get the story back to Australia on time.

Siege of the dressing room

'THEY KEPT STREAMING OVER THE GROUND LIKE A BATTLE SCENE FROM SOME ANCIENT HOLLYWOOD EPIC'

There has been a lot of drama in the cricket world in the past few years but the climax, for me, came in the early part of 1979 when I was chosen for my second tour of the West Indies.

Unlucky? Me? A second tour of the West Indies? I never thought I'd hear myself say that.

Yet it is true. I went there with the Australian World Series Cricket team, but the West Indies of 1979 just did not compare with the same place six years earler, and a series of events led up to the high drama of the Super Test in Georgetown, Guyana on the mainland of South America.

Georgetown is a difficult place to come to terms with, especially to those of us used to a conservative and stable political climate. There the politics are so far to the left that people go around calling each other "comrade". That sort of behavior is a bit of a shock to the system at first. And most of the time it is like Melbourne on a Sunday — dead!

In a climate like that, cricket plays a pretty important part in the thinking of most of the people. At the time of our arrival, they had not seen their local cricket heroes for nearly two years. Clive Lloyd, Colin Croft and Alvin Kallicharran are the next best thing to saints on their home ground, Bourda. With the advent of World Series Cricket, they had not been playing at home for a long time.

Then the first two days of the Super Test were lost due to rain.

But all the tickets for the match had been sold in block form, which is normal for West Indian centres, and those in India and Pakistan. That system means that the ticket-holder goes to the match for the full five days, for the price of the ticket.

That's fine, while the weather is, but when rain cuts the playing time back to three days, some of those holding block tickets are liable to get slightly upset. The cost of those tickets is equivalent to about a week's wages for the average worker in Guyana.

I suppose at nine o'clock on the third day some of the more experienced of us should have started to suspect that affairs might become a little lively. An hour before play was scheduled to start and even though we knew that wouldn't happen, there were thousands of people lining up to get inside the ground.

This farcical situation happened because the local administrators had announced to the media — and anyone else within earshot — that play would start on time.

People had begun arriving at the ground in the early hours of the morning and the gates had been opened at 7.30 a.m. to let in the human flood. Opening the gates, of course, just increased their expectations, and by the time we arrived, the mob was in a pretty good humour.

Attendance was heading towards capacity — about 25,000 (15,000 paying).

Like most grounds in the West Indies, the crowd was everywhere. On the terraces, in the stands, up in the palm trees, on the corrugated iron roofs of the stands and on the top of advertising boards. If only there had been the possibility of an early start. It was a sight to gladden the heart of any player.

Little umpire Douglas Sang Hue had been looking forward to an easy day. Even though he had been the subject of crowd riots earlier in his career, I don't think he suspected that a volcano was about to erupt.

The Australians were convinced that a cup of tea and quiet game of cards would be the only activity for most of the day. As 12th man, I wasn't grumbling much about that prospect.

That's not the way it turned out.

By the time the ground clock had got past two o'clock, much rum and coke had got down the throats of most of the crowd and the atmosphere was electric.

That was just the scenario for 'Lazarus' to make his entrance. I don't have the details on Lazarus, other than that he belonged to one of the fanatical religious sects that abound in the area and that he felt he had a direct line to the Almighty.

The first hint we got of the impending disaster was when this fellow came over the barbed wire fence, squelched his way through the sea of mud that was the outfield and ran up to the centre wicket area. He put on a great show there, going down on his knees and kissing the ground. Then, apparently quite harmless, he trotted across to the fence on the other side of the ground. Everyone in the ground had their eyes fixed on Lazarus —not the least of the reasons being that there was scarcely anything else to attract attention.

When he reached the area normally reserved for the steel band, Lazarus took a firm hold of the microphone and held up his hand for silence. There was not a sound, which, in the circumstances, was some performance. In an emotional, but very clear voice, he spoke: "I, Lazarus, have with the help of the Almighty One, been to the centre wicket."

Eyeballs rolling heavenwards, Lazarus continued: "The wicket is firm! The wicket is hard, it is true!"

Any fool could see that his statement was a load of rubbish, but even so, a shocked gasp ran through the crowd. Lazarus waited for absolute silence before he delivered his punchline: "And I, Lazarus tell you, THERE SHALL BE PLAY!"

The entire crowd, every last one of them, rose as one, roaring approval, jumping and shaking with joy. It was a sight I'll remember as long as I live.

Poor old Douglas Sang Hue was now forced into the position where the very least he could do was make another inspection of the wicket.

He edged out to the centre, doing his level best to be inconspicuous, then he made his way back to the pavilion, as fast as possible, without actually running. There was no need for any of us to ask the little umpire the verdict: his decision was written all over his face.

The boys in the outer indicated their feelings by taking hold of the large wooden posts that held up the barbed wire fence, and shaking as hard as they could; their friends behind them were busy throwing coke bottles on to the ground.

As an encore they grabbed hold of the portable steel seats they had been using and sent them flying over the fence like so many paper darts. Next door, in the double-storey public stand, they found a more ingenious method of mayhem. Solid timber seats, six to eight metres long, began to drop from the balcony on to the crowd below. Not just one or two. We counted in horror: 40 altogether.

How nobody was killed or maimed is something I'll never understand. When they finally ran out of ammunition, the ground on the lower level looked just as if a giant had been playing 'pick-up sticks'.

The lull was only temporary. The outer mob finally succeeded in uprooting the first of the posts supporting the barbed-wire. Down it went with a crash. The others went in quick succession, with a series of thuds —like a strike at ten-pin bowling. That started off a chain reaction around the ground, and posts and barbed wire fencing hit the ground.

That was the signal for 15,000 enraged cricket fans to storm the arena. They kept streaming over the ground, like a battle scene from some ancient Hollywood epic — only this time we weren't looking at celluloid.

But I felt like a film cameraman as I focused my favorite Canon camera. Like every other keen photographer, I had been praying for a situation like this all my life. I imagine a war correspondent at the front line would have the same feeling. I was scared stiff, but kept steadily clicking through a fortune in film.

At that stage, I was standing in front of the players' area — a place I naively thought was relatively safe. In front of me, a woman was hit by a bottle flush in her face. Her skin was laid wide open, blood splattered everywhere — a sickening sight.

The rest of the women were rushing for cover, but there was not much to be found. To the side of the players' area were two ladies' toilets about two metres by one metre each. There must have been at least 70 women crammed into that space — a good performance but I would have hated to be the one at the bottom of the pile.

There was a fellow near me, a huge bald West Indian who didn't seem at all aggressive. I'm sure he was just trying to find his way out of the place when a piece of four by two collided firmly with his forehead. It did not even break the skin, but just like a clip from a Three Stooges comedy, an enormous black lump appeared on his head and just kept growing and growing.

I was still clicking away, with the adrenalin pumping hard when, with a ghastly tinkling sound, the first of the windows above my head smashed in. For once my reflexes didn't let me down. I had the lens cap on and was back in the dressing room in a flash.

Just as I got inside, the room attendant — we believed he was a member of the military because of his green uniform and blackboots — was displaying some common sense. "Down! Get down! Get down!" he yelled and showed us the way with an acrobatic dive into a corner. It didn't take long for us to follow suit.

It could be said that the atmosphere was more than a little tense. We were in a room, which was scarcely more than a wooden hut, with big glass windows along two sides. Outside were thousands of deranged people screaming for blood — anybody's blood, but preferably that of a few Australian cricketers.

And they were throwing anything that moved. Bottles, stones, hunks of timber, bits of iron, came showering through the windows every couple of seconds. And with all that was a continuing hail of glass. From where we crouched, there was only one way out — and that wasn't very inviting. We

I imagine a war correspondent at the front line would have the same feeling . . .

couldn't get into the players' area because the mob was already in there. The only other door led to the West Indies' team room but that made no sense, they were in as much trouble as we were. So the only escape was through the windows — or what was left of them.

That theory didn't last long. We hadn't come dressed to go scrambling through a commando course of broken window panes and flying missiles — all we were wearing were shorts, T-shirts and thongs. At this point, someone decided discretion might be the better part of valour.

Most of us pulled on our best runners — and went back to a game of cards, in the hope the situation might quieten itself. Like the toothache, we were hoping that if we ignored it for long enough, it would go away.

Not all the players were as composed as that. Big Mick Malone, a giant of a man who played Australian Rules football in Perth, had wedged himself in a corner behind our room attendant. Team joker Gary Gilmour had chewed the ends from nine of his fingers and fainted. David Hookes, a young fellow with something to say about most things, hadn't spoken for 20 minutes! Unbelievable.

The riot sounded as if it was intensifying. That started us thinking about how best to protect ourselves and it wasn't long before everyone had pads strapped to their arms and donned their helmets. A couple even contemplated using their bats for purposes other than the makers had intended.

The fellow I really felt sorry for was Douglas Sang Hue. If the mob recognised him, there wouldn't be much money around to say that he would come out of it alive.

Douglas' main problem was his size — when he stands on tip-toe, his eyes are about level with Joel Garner's kneecaps. Disguise was going to be difficult for him. Instead, he pulled a towel over his head, not in protection against the flying objects, but in the hope that the rioters wouldn't realise who he was.

Then one wall of our room began to shake as if a big earth tremor was in progress. It didn't take long for us to work out the riot had spread to the bar next door. We could hear the glasses thudding and shattering against the walls; the pictures torn down and smashed to pieces; the trophies looted. About the only glass not broken, we discovered later, was that which held the scotch, rum, brandy and other spirits. Even rampaging mobs have respect for the important things in life.

Outside again, steel chairs started flying through the air, along with anything else in reach.

Now, we were firmly wedged into a corner. Dennis Lillee was so near the bottom of the pile of bodies that all I could see of him were the soles of his running shoes. It might have been uncomfortable there but I think anybody else in the team would have been happy to swap with him.

Lennie Pascoe was just swaying backwards and forwards not sure whether to attack or defend.

We had stacked our cricket bags against the door in the hope they would form some sort of barrier to the mob. The realisation was starting to get through to us that our lives were in serious danger. In a word, we were terrified.

It is almost funny to recall now what went through my mind in those moments — but it was a long way from being humorous at the time. I began to think of all the things I had done in my lifetime that I shouldn't have; all the things that I hadn't done that I should have — silly things like "Why hadn't I ever been to Disneyland?" What a lousy way to go — trampled to death in a little timber shed in Georgetown, Guyana.

Some of the good points flashed through my mind too.

I had played a fair bit of Test cricket, been to many countries of the world. I had even read Frank Tyson's *Victorian Cricket Association Coaching Manual* — although there wasn't an awful lot in that about how to defend yourself against a bottle-wielding mob, while dressed in shorts, T-shirt and a World Series batting helmet!

Suddenly, six shots rang out!!!!!!

We had no way of telling who fired them, or who was the target — none of us were particularly interested to find out. For what was supposed to be a game of cricket had turned into something more like World War 3.

Then the door caved in. I nearly fainted with fright, and I had a few mates.

Through the opening came five of the biggest militiamen imaginable, with sub-machine guns slung from their shoulders. "Get down, get down!" the first of them yelled. My first reaction was that we were going to be part of an Entebbe-type rescue mission.

The tension broke as the militiamen started laughing and pointed. "Hey man, look! Look at that!"

We scrambled to get a view as about 50 of their militia mates charged across the pitch — perspex shields, truncheons and sub-machine guns at the ready, as the yahoos ran for their lives. I can't blame them. I wouldn't have been stopping to ask if the boys in green had orders to shoot.

It was a wonderful feeling to have those militiamen on our side. What a riot! What a day!

Take my wife, please

'EVERYTIME SHE LAUGHED, WHICH WAS OFTEN, THE STAND SHOOK'

The West Indies cricketers have captured the hearts and imagination of cricket lovers throughout the world with their own wonderful brand of Calypso cricket. Yet my first encounter with West Indies cricket during the official 1973 Australian Tour did not really fulfil my somewhat fanciful expectations of the game in the Caribbean.

The first match against the Under-23 team of Jamaica was played under very primitive conditions. There were no boundary lines marked on the ground and at various intervals during play, water buffalo, black goats and cows wandered on to the playing field to make a closer inspection of proceedings. And above, vultures with 1.5-metre wingspans hovered ominously.

A crudely constructed tin shed with rusty nails for clothes hooks was the dressing room. Some people reckon representing your country in sport is all glamour — forget it!

Rum-drinking spectators used the outside of the corrugated iron shed as a urinal. The stench was overpowering.

I was fascinated by the fervour of the West Indians, particularly for their cricket. Everywhere the Aussie team went we were followed by admirers and autograph seekers. They were anxious for a glimpse of Dennis Lillee, whose reputation as one of the most formidable bowlers in the world had preceded him to the islands.

At the airport the West Indians chanted and hissed their acclamation. "Where's Lillee, man? Let's see the tiger. Let the tiger loose, man. Where is he man? Which one's Lillee?"

The boisterous adulation of Lillee irked Kerry O'Keeffe, one of the three leg spinners in our team. He was often disappointed that he was never recognised by the fans.

But once, at Georgetown airport, his chest was puffed out and he was flushed with pride when he heard a very loud chorus: "Which one's O'Keeffe man. Where's the blond leggy, man? Let O'Keeffe loose man."

Later he was more than just a little put out to learn that Rod Marsh and myself had led and encouraged the chorus. He has never forgiven me.

I was startled by the smallness of the Test grounds and the forbidding three metre-high barbed wire fences which encircled the playing areas. I was told it was to keep us in and had nothing to do with the crowd!

My first Test match was just incredible. The ground at Sabina Park, Kingston, Jamaica, could only hold about 15,000 or so spectators at capacity, but there must have been at least 25,000 there on every day. They were packed in so tight that you could see the barbed wire fence move in and out as they breathed, and the big light pylons were almost totally covered by people by 11 a.m. each morning.

And to think here in Australia we worry about getting a corrugated bum sitting on the timber-slatted seats at the MCG and other grounds.

I remember the crowd was even hanging over the brick walls. Two of these five metre-high walls, painted pale green, were in fact the sight-screens. And such was the size of the ground that Dennis Lillee marked his run-up from just underneath the overhanging toes of the spectators.

When Lillee pushed off the wall to bowl, all 25,000 fans began this eerie chant. It came from the bottom of the throat and built into an enormous crescendo. But strangely it stopped abruptly in the fast bowler's delivery stride and there was a deathly silence around the ground.

Dennis was bowling to Roy Fredericks, and like most left-handers, against Lillee he played and missed the first ball.

As the ball went past the outside face of his bat, the whole 25,000 breathed in all at once, emitting an extraordinary wind-rushing sound. I can honestly say it was so draughty at fine leg I had trouble getting my trousers off the barbed wire fence. It was really incredible stuff.

And this continued ball after ball.

Playing cricket in front of West Indian crowds was a magnificent experience, particularly for a specialist fine leg and third man fielder — it was certainly a job that I failed, unlike Roger Harper, to turn into a glamour position. Nevertheless, I had a lot of fun there.

That Test match at Sabina Park was my first on overseas soil. I can still remember the crowd's reaction as I walked back to my position at fine leg after successfully taking the wicket of century maker Maurice Foster. Not one of them was smiling and all I could see was the glistening three metre barbed wire fence!

Some guy screamed out "Wokka, you bad man Wokka!!!" I froze. It must be clearly understood that some of these blokes can really throw a coke bottle. In fact most of them could land a bottle, rock or whatever on to the centre wicket area without any trouble.

Lots of players, even today, and particularly specialist close-to-the-wicket fielders are terrified about fielding on the fence.

They will walk the last 30 or so metres backwards and that's not really what the crowds want. They demand generally some form of communication or eye contact with a player close to them.

Finally, later in the afternoon, I found one guy alone who was a bit of a wrap for me. "Wokka, Wokka, if you get one more wicket you can have my wife," he yelled.

I didn't want to look but I did. Sure enough, high up on the bamboo seats at the back row of the stand was a guy with his arm around his wife.

They're very long-limbed fellows these West Indians, and I must admit this guy was struggling to get his fingertips around his wife's shoulders.

She was huge! She could have been the lady on the front of the 'Black Mammy' self-raising flour packet. This was her sitting up in the stand. She had about two teeth, closely cropped hair, and enormous gold ear-rings. Everytime she laughed, which was often, the stand shook. Finally she smiled at me. It would be fair to say the lady was not pretty.

"You like?" The big man roared above the crowd. I noted the guy had a lot of mates and of course I liked, eh? If ever I needed a lefthander to come to the wicket so I could get across to the other side of the ground, this was the moment!

I was so worried about taking another wicket. I had visions of leaving the ground after play and seeing this giant of a man, muscles on muscles, with a cane-cutting knife shining in the moonlight, saying "Here she is man, she's yours!"

I did take a few more wickets to finish with six for the innings, yet fortunately my path was unimpeded as I left the field that evening. My imagination had run riot by stumps.

Everytime she laughed, which was often, the stand shook.

Cabbie for a Day
'THEY KNOW EVERYTHING, WELL THEY USED TO'

Have you been disappointed in the local knowledge and performance of your cab driver recently? I have been!

In fact I wonder how some of the characters driving taxis these days get past the initial screening test — maybe there's no such thing as a screening test? Certainly there doesn't appear to be any driver education before setting them loose on an unsuspecting public.

When I get in a cab, I expect the driver to have a pretty good idea of where I want to go . . . but I've run into a couple of real live ones.

Three times in Sydney during last summer I told the man behind the steering wheel of my cab, "Sydney Cricket Ground, driver!"

Can you believe they didn't know where the SCG was!

I'm still looking for the last English-speaking taxi driver in Sydney — maybe he's out of work. I certainly haven't seen him but I wish he'd come back to work.

Cabbies are generally a fascinating group of people — so full of life's stories and always a wealth of gossip to make the journey pass quickly . . . they know everything. Well, they used to. You could name a subject and they knew about it, name a place and they'd either have been there or had a fellow you are talking about in their cab. You want a few suggestions on where to go or what to do in a strange town — no question, ask a taxi driver. Today that philosophy would be a bit of a gamble!

Once they used to know their cities inside out. From the back streets to all the bright city lights. I think that still is the case in London — they must be the best in the world. Before a licence is granted in London the applicant must undergo a minimum two-year apprenticeship or qualifying period.

It's not just a case of $100,000 plus . . . changing hands for a pair of plates as is the case here in Australia.

But don't get me wrong, I've had some bad rides overseas too!

I'll never forget driving, yes, driving a beat up old cab back from Pointe Pierre some 60 miles to Port of Spain, the capital of Trinidad, in 1973.

It was during the official Australian cricket tour of the Caribbean and hire-buses were a bit scarce over there. The cabs were appropriately called Taboo Taxis! Don't laugh.

Our manager Bill Jacobs had no option but to organise five of these magnificent 'stock-cars' — the only thing they lacked were the large graphic numbers to distinguish each car from other 'race' competitors. And they had the hide to ask money from passengers.

Honestly you would need danger money to hop in with some of these guys. On the narrow stretch of highway — two lanes — between Port of Spain and Pointe Pierre some 115 people had been killed.

I noticed the gum trees were getting taller and more plentiful.

Unfortunately we had to invite the five cab drivers to attend the cricket match while waiting to take us back to town. No man loves a rum like a West Indian cricket enthusiast and these guys were no different.

In the time between 10 a.m. and 7.30 p.m., when we wished to leave, all five drivers were particularly under the weather — they'd all had a truck load of the local dark rum! And with devastating effect.

It really was a gamble which cab I ought to travel in . . . like three other cricketers, I made a bad choice in settling for the first cab.

Being long in the legs I grabbed the front, or death seat, in the beat up old Datsun . . . circa 1960. In the back seat huddled — Kerry O'Keeffe, Greg Chappell and Dennis Lillee.

After nearly flooding the engine at take-off, our man drove like a man possessed.

Initially, we ran over six successive 'sleeping policemen' or speed traps at 50 mph just getting out of the surrounds . . . a bit quick considering the car had no suspension left at all.

Then it was straight through the centre point of a primitive sand-bagged roundabout and on to the other side. He didn't apologise because he had the hiccups and couldn't speak. I thought he may be sick — it had been a rough ride.

Finally we got to a T-intersection with a view to turning right. No giving way . . . that would have been too easy. Straight out into the mainstream traffic almost running an oncoming car road off the road.

At this stage enough was enough!!

I asked him to stop the car after much backseat urging. He just laughed and started waving his arms around.

I'm sure he had not bathed in a week . . . the smell of stale perspiration on the short sleeve, bri-nylon shirt was sickening each time he lifted his arms to expose his hairy armpits.

As he laughed he turned his wrinkled face to look straight at me . . . his breath was like a flame thrower of pure alcohol.

Finally he stopped at our insistence.

I noticed the overhead wires strung between lonely telegraph poles at the point where we had stopped was the resting place for these huge birds. They may have been vultures . . . very bright red necks, no feathers, a decidedly droopy look about their bodies and exaggerated hooked beaks. It was almost as if they were waiting for an accident to happen . . . well, they hadn't been let down in the past.

After much discussion about the number of children our driver had sired and the necessity to maintain his job, he eventually swapped places with me.

This bloke lasted just three or four minutes in the co-pilot's seat before passing out on us . . . like a light, dead to the world.

I've driven some bad motor cars in my time but this one had to be the worst I've ever attempted to move . . . even worse than my first motor car, a pale grey, 1951 Vauxhall which I purchased for $25, including registration.

Changing gears on the cab was about as successful as pulling the lever on a poker machine . . . much criticism was emanating from the back seat!!

Meanwhile our driver slept on and on and on! Some 75 minutes later we arrived back at the Queen's Park Hotel where we were being accommodated.

We never did pay that fellow but by the time he woke up I'm sure he wondered whether it was just a bad dream.

But at least we arrived at our destination! That wasn't the case in Sydney just a few months ago!

I was expected at a shopping promotion at Mt Druid about 30 km from the GPO. The Hilton Hotel concierge suggested the trip might take 50-60 minutes.

My driver on this occasion looked like he was on holiday from Taiwan. And he might well have been judging by his local knowledge . . . there was a very real chance of us both getting lost.

After remaining calm and quiet for approximately 45 minutes, travelling well away from town, I began to get anxious! Not only about the time but also about the number of well-grazed paddocks standing four or five horses and lots of dairy cows. Also I noticed the gum trees were getting taller and more plentiful — bush I would call it.

Then, from the back seat I observed the hapless driver rotating the street directory from left to right . . . I'm sure he didn't know where north was, let alone the city! That little black arrow was moving up and down on the seat like the gauge of his speedometer.

Finally, after some very heavy cross-examination, he actually admitted he was lost . . . we hadn't seen a major street sign for about 10 minutes. We were in big trouble!

Gee I was upset — I had definitely missed my 10 a.m. store appearance and I'd let down all of the people who had turned up to talk to me, not to mention the client who organised the exercise — he now had egg on his face!

I asked my friend to pull up at the nearest petrol station and gave him $10 — the meter said $44.70. I told him to find his own way back to the city if he could! Maybe I was a bit stronger with my words but I was not happy!

These days when I hail a cab I do so with a great deal of apprehension . . . it's a joy to run into someone who really knows his way around, can chat a bit about cricket and footy and who likes a laugh. After all, like any business you can't expect to get paid if you don't offer the customer service!

Hunted by a Bargain
'WE WERE ADVISED NOT TO LEAVE THE HOTEL'

I am always looking for bargains, and I have a few lovely paintings at home which I collected after hours of bargain-hunting in London a few years ago. So, when I am home, I gaze at them smugly.

Unhappily, looking at that beautiful art also reminds me of an occasion when I was really suckered. That was in Kingston, Jamaica, on a tour of the West Indies in 1979, when I just couldn't refuse a none-too-affable giant who insisted that I purchase his wares.

Actually, if I had taken the advice of local officials, I wouldn't have been walking the streets anyway. Kingston wasn't what you would call a tourist haven, and because of the political trouble at the time, we were advised not to leave the hotel. But, after a couple of days in this prison, we decided to go out in groups of four or five, and we survived.

Of course, we encountered pros, pimps, pushers and pedlars every few metres, but we had the numbers and our fixed grins to protect us.

One night, as a group of us headed to a restaurant recommended by one of our players — he had obviously something against us because it was awful tucker — I came across my 6ft. 9in. salesman.

As we walked along the street, where lights are seemingly a mile apart and dark alleys come up every couple of steps, I felt a huge hand latch onto my shoulder and drag me into one alley. All I could see was flashing eyes, and he was so big, I couldn't even look him straight in the eye.

He gave me the usual line — he had 10 kids and five brothers to feed and unless I bought some of his goods, they would surely starve. Then, he unwrapped a filthy rag and displayed four sparkling gold bracelets. He claimed they were 14 carat gold, and said, no insisted, that I buy the four bracelets for $35 Australian.

I figured they were phoney, but I just couldn't shake this bloke. When I challenged him about where he got them, he told me the story of broken cases at the Kingston wharves, where the locals feel it is imperative that "Nothing which hits the ground should be left there."

I finally broke his grip, and said I wasn't interested. But he warned me that he wouldn't go away and that I would eventually buy his goods.

We ate and then strolled back towards the hotel. You wouldn't believe it, this giant grabbed me off the street again.

I was fed up, and told him I only had $17 on me. He grabbed the money, handed me the bracelets and disappeared.

I sold two of them to a couple of players and was pleasantly surprised when I inspected the other two in my room. Not bad at all, I thought, make wonderful presents.

I didn't give the bloke another thought until a few days later when he was waiting in the foyer of the hotel. There were security guards there, so he organised a meeting in the gents.

This time, he had another six gold bracelets and rather than argue —actually this time I was rather keen — I paid $20 for the lot. What a bargain I thought to myself. Almost all of my presents already bought for just $37.

However, a few weeks later, they appeared to be losing their sheen, and by the time I arrived home they were green and blotchy. I had been done easily and I still curse that giant in the back alley of Kingston.

I still can't figure out how he made it into the hotel foyer, such is the security at most hotels in the Caribbean.

Actually, a hotel foyer provided another funny incident during my playing days. It was in South Africa in 1975 when I toured with a Derek Robins XI. One of the guest players was John Shepherd, the West Indian Test all-rounder, who also was so successful with Kent in English county cricket, and with Footscray in Victorian District cricket.

He was standing in the foyer of the Newlands Hotel, wearing his touring team uniform. Unfortunately, the blazers were remarkably similar to those worn by the staff of the hotel, and 'Shep' looked just like a porter as he stood there with his sparkling smile.

A lady straight from the blue-rinse set, arrived and plonked her two suitcases at Shepherd's feet. "Take these to room 505, if you please," she commanded. Shepherd didn't miss a beat and said: "Seeing we are neighbours, it will be a pleasure, because I am in room 506."

That really stunned the old dear, who demanded to know what he was talking about, telling her that he was her neighbor. "Haven't you heard, lady? The government has changed its policy, and blacks have become honorary whites for the next three weeks," Shepherd said as he walked away to the breakfast room, leaving the stunned lady shocked and her suitcases stranded.

Shepherd was fantastic in the climate, and helped unite the separate groups. It wasn't easy considering the apartheid problem, but he never lost his sense of humour.

One day we were travelling through Soweto looking at the poverty and wondering about the future of South Africa. "Don't worry, we are about to take the place over, and I will be the Minister of Youth, Sport and Recreation. And don't worry, Maxie, I will get you a job in one of the gardens," he joked.

In one game there were the usual separate dressingrooms. Not 'amateurs' and 'professionals' as in the old days in England, but 'whites' and 'blacks'. Shepherd went into the black room, and I joined him for the company. We hammered a couple of nails into the wall for hangers, and proceeded to get ready for the match.

Another bloke who found life in South Africa rather strange was Malcolm Franke, the Sri Lankan, who played so much cricket for Queensland.

Now Malcolm would be the first to admit he has an all-year suntan, which had never caused him the slightest embarrassment. In fact, he was proud of it. But in South Africa you had to be either black or white, and he had difficulty figuring exactly where he stood.

So, whenever he gave an autograph, he wrote 'Australia' in brackets beside it.

Yes, there are many memories as I look at these paintings from England.

He had 10 kids and five brothers to feed.

Chapter Six

SEEING THE FUNNY SIDE

Echoes of the MCG

'AS ONE MEMBER DIED, THEY MOVED UP BY ONE PLACE'

The Melbourne Cricket Ground means many things to many people. As for myself, I seem to have spent the greater part of my adult life tenaciously linked to the sacred piece of dirt — my destiny finely balanced in the hands of the Melbourne Football Club selectors initially, and later, the gentlemen who were to show faith in my ability to play cricket, first for Melbourne, then Victoria and finally Australia.

My first taste of life at the MCG was as a guest of the Melbourne Football Club to watch the 1966 VFL grand final between St Kilda and Collingwood.

More than 100,000 fans were there. As the national anthem, God Save The Queen, began to play over the loudspeakers, an enormous roar broke out from the crowd. At that stage I think I made a commitment to myself . . . I knew I wanted to be part of this marvellous place.

Three months later, accompanied by my father, 'Big Max', I returned to the MCG as a potential VFL footballer for the Melbourne club.

I remember the long walk around the dark tunnel, below the MCG seating, to the football club dressing rooms.

The legendary coach, Norm Smith, and the prince of VFL club secretaries (I guess I'm allowed a little bias) Jim Cardwell had escorted us to the green dressing room door.

Before I entered a new phase of my life, Norm turned to my dad and said, "This is where you get off. From now on he's mine. All you have to do for Max is to keep his hair cut!"

Next he glanced at me and stated, "By the way son, these are the Melbourne Football Club changing rooms and not the dressing sheds."

I laughed to myself, but kept a straight face as I thought of some of the cold and draughty excuses for dressing sheds in Tasmania that I had returned to after playing my heart out — only to be greeted with the news of, "Cold showers tonight, boys."

Time passed quickly as the smell of linament lured me towards the big time. I got my chance with just seven games of the 1967 season remaining — against North Melbourne at the MCG.

The moment of truth came ever so quickly as I stood opposite the giant North Melbourne ruckman, Noel Teasdale.

The next thing I remember was laying flat on my back a few yards from the centre circle, not an ounce of air in my lungs, looking upward at the beautifully formed cumulo nimbus clouds. I knew at that precise moment that VLF football was not going to be easy. But that is another story.

Ninety-four VFL games later the time seemed right to stop. I'd been selected to play Test cricket against Pakistan in the second Test of the 1972-73 season.

But in the meantime, as a student of architecture at the Royal Melbourne Institute of Technology, I was to spend most of my holidays as a member of the maintenance staff at the MCG.

Looking back I reckon I must have painted 40,000 seats in the MCG. Firstly we had to clean the timber seating planks, then we applied the red-lead orange base coat, two coats of green and finally the more difficult task of stencilling on all the seat numbers.

My mentor in those days was a great guy, Joe Kinnear, a sportsman in his own right but as a scoreboard operator he never missed a VFL game in some 40 years. He was a pretty hard man but had a great sense of humour, generally at my expense.

After I had displayed an unusual amount of ability with a paint brush in my first two weeks, Joe decided it was time for me to accept some responsibility — a sort of promotion, more like an elevation actually.

Joe had delegated me the task of painting two flag poles on the Members' Stand roof.

White was about the colour of my face as I craned my neck to view those two lonely flagpoles, perched 150 ft above on the corners of the old corrugated iron roof. It appeared that the only thing supporting the base of the poles was the guttering at the front edge of the roof.

Nevertheless, equal to the task, I soon found myself brush in pocket, paint tin in hand and ladder between myself and the pole, peering over the edge of the roof to the sound of laughter below.

It was Joe explaining to an audience of groundsmen and maintenance staff what a precarious position I now happened to be in — and that he had no real intention of me painting the poles!

Over a period of many years Joe and I became great friends. The Melbourne Cricket Club acknowledged his service with life membership.

We talked often of cricket and football, especially during the first class cricket matches held at the MCG. Then it was our job to operate the old scoreboard — the Jack Fingleton Scoreboard now occupying a new site at the Manuka Oval in Canberra.

The long room at the MCG is perhaps the best place in the ground to view a game from. It is a very historic space, steeped in nostalgia and choked in tradition.

History expresses itself in all forms within this room as does a certain code of ethics — and not just for sportsmen.

After playing a hard game of Aussie rules for the Melbourne reserves it was suggested that several of us younger players should watch the senior game from the long room.

We arrived dressed in blazer, tie and grey trousers, as was the club policy, at the end of the first quarter. To my delight I found three vacant seats on a huge brown leather couch positioned directly in front of the glass viewing area.

Not to miss an opportunity like this, I sat down quickly as did my two team-mates. After a short stay, my left ankle was tapped very formally with a cane walking stick extending from the hand of a very stooped old gentleman. He must have been 90.

He explained in a rather croaky voice that I was in his seat and he had been occupying the same place or close to it for many, many years.

Embarrassed, my mates and I left rather sheepishly to later find out that the seating on that couch was traditionally for only the oldest members of the MCC.

As one member died, they all moved up by one place to their left. I had obviously occupied the oldest club member's seat!

Memories easily come flooding back again . . . like painting the seats in the outer at the MCG below the Southern Stand. It had been a long hot day under the Melbourne sun.

It was about 3 p.m. and I hadn't had much rest. I explained to my boss, Joe, that I had a bad bellyache and I needed nature to take its course.

Joe suggested the ladies' toilets beneath the grandstand would be the quickest, and that was OK as it was only a weekday afternoon.

Seconds later I was seated in one of the cubicles in the women's conveniences.

I looked around the walls, deep in thought . . . the graffiti was unreal!

The silence was broken by the sound of footsteps coming towards my door. I immediately extended my foot to the base of the door in nervous fashion.

I breathed a sigh of relief as the adjoining door slammed shut. But how was I going to get out? How long would I sit there?

In those days, the toilet paper holders were fixed to the column between two doors. I thought, what happens if I put my hand out the door at the same time as the lady next door . . . fortunately it didn't eventuate and I completed the 'paperwork'.

Then I bolted as fast as I could, holding back my nervous laughter until I was safely outside.

I couldn't wait to tell Joe and the others what had happened . . . they laughed a lot.

Then, Dave, one of Joe's offsiders arrived on the scene ten minutes later with a story about disturbing a woman in the ladies' toilets below the Southern grandstand!

The Day of my First Kick
'DOWN I WENT LIKE A BAG OF WET CEMENT'

It is pretty natural for a young fella of eight years old to spend most of his school day gazing out the classroom window. I was no exception. Like almost every boy in my grade, I wanted to be a VFL footballer and I also wanted to be a Test cricketer — as a batsman!

Now there is nothing wrong with dreaming, in fact, all man's greatest inventions and achievements have been a direct result of dreaming. Someone once said, "What can be conceived and believed in the mind can be achieved in reality." This philosophy remains the basis for all positive thinking.

I was too young at the time to realise that those wonderful childhood dreams were the beginnings of a process that was later to become second nature in future sporting endeavours: all of these dreams were on a big wide screen, rich in colour, full of familiar sounds like whistles, sometimes painful physical clashes and never too far away from the smell of linament!

At night, just before dropping off to sleep, I would shut my eyes and visualise playing my first game of VFL football. In those days there were no video cassette recorders or computers. In fact, Hobart didn't receive the technology of television until 1960, four years after the 1956 Olympic Games in Melbourne.

In these days of high technology, I still believe that the best computers in the world are not the big ones from IBM, Digital or Data General, but the one between our ears. Everyone is responsible for the pictures seen on their own screens and it's definitely your own fault if you get bad images in your head.

Anyway, I used to imagine getting my first kick in VFL football somewhere near the members' wing on the MCG, in front of 70,000 screaming fans. The dream was always consistent. The struggle of gaining possession, then the kick!

The kick was the easy part — just a matter of putting the football, lace-upwards, gently to the ground. You see, drop kicks were my specialty, whereas today they are non-existent. A player would be dragged from the ground by his coach and fined $1000 for even attempting one.

That wasn't the case during my dreams in the 50's. Nightly, I used to feel the bag of wind make perfect contact with my highly polished boot (my dad used to say, 'Even if you can't play the game, at least look as if you can'). The resultant energy would propel the football spectacularly, end over end, some 65 metres onto the half-forward line where a team-mate would stand on an opponent's head to take the mark of the day.

Then the members stand would rise as one to applaud my efforts. Dressed in their grey, gabardine overcoats and with cigar smoke creating a blue grey haze above their heads, they would continue to clap like mad. Gee, I used to enjoy getting that kick!

I must honestly say that almost a decade later, when I realised my ambition of playing VFL football, my first kick didn't come so easily.

It was 1967 when I made my debut in senior football for the Melbourne Football Club. With only seven games of the season remaining, I'd finally got my chance against North Melbourne at the MCG.

I was the last player selected on Melbourne's supplementary list for the year and subsequently was given guernsey No. 46. Yours truly was so skinny in those days (12 st 9lbs or about — 79kg) that the '4' started just under my left armpit and the '6' finished under my right. Embarrassingly, I ran down the race in a short-sleeved jumper — my 'suntan' in the middle of winter could be described as 'polar bear white' and my elbows were like razor blades.

Halfback flanker Don Williams was playing his 200th game but I was so excited, I didn't know whether the team was lining up in ceremony for his 200th or for my first! I charged through the large red and blue banner and jogged a couple of laps to soak up the atmosphere. It was great until just before the start of the contest . . . There I was in the middle of the fabulous Melbourne Cricket Ground. The umpire held the ball aloft in one hand and drew the tiny stainless steel container to his lips with the other.

Then I noticed the guy standing opposite me in the blue and white striped jumper — Noel Teasdale. A giant, barrel-chested man, almost 17 stone (108 kg). On his forehead he wore a leather patch which protected a metal plate inside his skull, the legacy of an old wound. To me the patch looked like it was holding his brains intact! I didn't tell him that at the time, he had a big weight advantage and they hadn't even bounced the ball.

Off went the siren, down went the ball and around went the pea in the whistle.

It should be understood that at 18 years of age, Maxwell Henry Norman Walker was a willowy, high leaping young fella from the Apple Isle. With eyes firmly fixed on the ball, I charged at the centre circle and leapt high in the air for the knockout, so high in fact that a copper on the boundary line later tried to book me for 'Loitering in the air'! Unfortunately it wasn't high enough!

Just as my hand made contact with the footy, Teasdale's huge frame crashed into mine with catastrophic results. He punched the ball about 40 metres towards his goal and sent No. 46 for the Demons about 25 metres in the same direction.

There I was lying flat on my back and gasping in the middle of the MCG with not an ounce of wind in my lungs and wondering what in bloody hell had hit me. I opened my eyes and remember seeing some beautifully shaped cumulo-nimbus clouds floating overhead. It was then that I realised league football is not going to be easy.

Nothing in the world beats perseverance . . . so I persevered.

Five minutes of the quarter had elapsed when the ball went over the boundary line in front of the smokers grandstand on the wing for a throw-in. I then remembered what the legendary coach, Norm Smith, had told me before the game: "Youu're a big kid son, make them climb over you!"

So I took his advice. Immediately I used my edge in natural pace to gain front possie and knock the pill down to rover and captain Hassa Mann who had a baulk, a weave and bounce or two before dobbing a magnificent goal.

At this stage I thought to myself, 'How long has this game been going on? You little beauty!' and headed back to the centre circle for the bounce-up. Teasdale jogged level with me and whispered bluntly, "If you get in front once more, I'll knock your so and so head right off your shoulder blades!"

Now, why should I believe this gorilla with the headgear? I'd heard similar comments from others and all to no avail. Without thinking too much more about his threat, I later prepared to contest another boundary throw — on the members wing again.

No worries, front position came easily to me. I got my hand on the ball beautifully to palm it down to Hassa, but then it happened. Whack! Right in the back of the neck. I pulled up inside the white boundary line with my chin firmly implanted in the moist turf.

"Play on!" was the call by the umpire. 'Gee, a bloke can be stiff, I thought, 'No free kick.' Remember too, I hadn't had my first kick yet! Still, I was prepared to give my ugly opponent the benefit of the doubt. But how could anyone clobber his opposition ruckman that hard on purpose and get away with it?

Lady luck wasn't smiling on me at all, because the footy had trickled only 20 metres before rolling over the line and out of bounds!

Being a creative big man, I thought about the possibility of still taking front position but instead decided to nudge the ball out to nippy winger Stanley Alves at the back of the pack . . . and it would've been great! But little did I realise that 'Tesser' had no time for creativity. This time he got me with a 'coat hanger' (elbow) behind the left ear! Down I went like a bag of wet cement, with church bells ringing inside my head. Seconds later the umpire nearly burst my right ear-drum by bending down and pronouncing he was awarding me a free kick!

Like a flash, out came Sam Alico, the MFC runner. "Kick it, kick it . . . !' he demanded. He must have thought I was Superman because my legs had buckled under me. Sam's strong hands supported me under each armpit. A kick was still out of the question. Maybe a handball?

Suddenly, Sam dug deep into his trouser pocket. Like most trainers who've been around a while, Sammy had a small packet of 'smelling salts'.

The lid was off the packet and under my nose it went. It was terrible but it did the job and my subsequent handball did reach a Melbourne player.

I was beginning to wonder whether or not I'd ever get a kick in this game . . .

While recovering in the back pocket, my dream came true at about the 11 minute mark of the first quarter. I attacked the ball as it cleared the halfback line. It was about to bounce about two metres in front of me. Which way would it bounce? Fortunately for me, it hit me fair and square on the left nipple! Here was my big chance!

There it was, safe in my possession. I held it at arm's length and looked . . . MATCH II, Tom Sherrin, rawhide leather . . . made in Australia. The real thing!

Now for the kick . . . blue and white jumpers everywhere, not much time, unlike in the technicolour dream in the computer of my mind, the memorable first kick was a wobbly old flat punt that travelled about 35 metres.

Whatever it looked like didn't really matter. I'll remember that kick for the rest of my life, simply because it was my first!

In Fright of the Drill
'IT WAS TOO LATE, THE CAVITIES WERE THERE'

Dentists may occupy one of the highest paid professions in the community, but to the average bloke in the street, I am pretty sure they are still looked upon as the 'fang snatcher' — a person with the ability to inflict unforgettable pain at will!

Then, after reducing the helpless patient to a frightened and crumpled shadow, they'll explain with a toothy smile, that the ordeal was necessary for your own good — a piercingly painful penalty for not looking after your teeth.

Of course, my pain threshold is somewhere around my ankles when it comes to the dentist . . . I can withstand a fair amount of pain (like any self-respecting man should) in broken noses, bruises, cuts and the like, but the intensely focused shrill that ricochets off the inside of one's skull and rebounds into the extremities, reduces me to the stature of a 'Mr. Puniverse' if a nerve is touched.

When I look back on an erratic career of visiting these white-coated gentlemen, many things have changed . . . but the same old pain occurs when they tweak a nerve!

My first visit to the dentist was as a small boy in Hobart. Ether was used to put me to sleep — I can still feel my head beginning to blow up like a football bladder and the glare of the lights above the antique barber's chair spinning around frantically like a Ferris wheel at night!

A couple of years later chloroform was used instead of ether . . . this was much better, but when the bad teeth had been extracted, the clotted blood and the gaping flesh were still a constant source of attention for my probing tongue!

In those days the chairs had arms, but not any more. During my visit to the dentist earlier this month, I discovered the hard way that they were missing — maybe he got sick of paying for repairs to the regularly dismembered chair!

I was excited by my dentist's poster on the ceiling, strategically placed directly above the head-rest on the reclining chair — something different to occupy my mind this visit!

As usual the large protective bib was placed around my neck as I tensely

groped for somewhere comfortable to support my awkward arms. I opted for the folded arms and clenched fist position and braced myself ready for the systematic 'scraping of the teeth' ritual that precedes all drilling.

Dentists tell you not to clean or pick your teeth with sharp metal objects. So what do they do? Probe every little crack and crevice with a miniature stainless-steel spike.

How do they know where the cavity is? They judge by the height their patient jumps off his chair as the exposed nerve is prodded. Sometimes that exploration into the plaque is more hurtful than the drilling and filling.

At this stage the nurse in uniform appears and some friendly three-way chatter occurs . . . maybe an X-ray is necessary?

Then comes the CRUNCH . . . how many fillings, and where?

In my case it was two — perhaps I'd been drinking too much Coca Cola. Anyway it was too late, the cavities were there.

My worst fears came true when he suggested a needle! I tried to shut my eyes before he produced the painkilling injection . . . but I failed!

There it was, a dirty big syringe with thumb cocked on the plunger ready to squirt its contents deep into my jaw bone — the fine metal needle on the end looked about 75mm long and even a bit blunt! My anxiety level trebled as the plastic cylinder hovered above my head like a sputnik in space.

"It might hurt a bit . . . and it might make your eyes water," the dentist suggested.

He should have said, "It's going to hurt and it'll certainly make your eyes water!"

Into the flesh went the needle — first to the left of my two upper front teeth, then direct hits above each of those and finally a fourth jab to the upper jaw.

I could have sworn the second plunge of pain-killer was buried deep enough to touch my sinuses . . . simultaneously a pair of huge elephant sized tears rolled off the assembly line in each tear duct.

Slowly my upper lip, plus my moustache, appeared to float right off my face . . . yes, the painkiller was definitely working.

I know it's easier if you're relaxed, but somehow my whole body seemed tensed up and my tightly clenched fists had 'white knuckle fever'.

Now for the drilling! Ready, aim . . . contact! I search for the expected pain but none is forthcoming. Maybe, just maybe, it won't hurt.

What feels like huge boulders of broken tooth, drop into the saliva that has been secreted into the region beneath my tongue . . . then the watchful nurse puts her stainless steel-tipped sucker hose to work. Like an underwater vacuum cleaner, the by-products of drilling soon disappear into the hose.

Once the decay has been removed only a gaping hole remains!

"Rinse!" says the dentist.

I nervously pick up the glass of pale pink liquid and attempt to swirl it around inside my mouth without spilling a drop, but as we all know, that's almost impossible when you haven't got an upper lip. Like a baby, dribble runs rapidly and embarrassingly from each corner of my mouth.

Next task is to spit the remaining rinse into what looks like a miniature bidet — the smell reminds me of formalin and the city morgue!

Back to the reclining position . . . the nurse is mixing the filler paste somewhere away from my eye line . . . the dentist rams the first wad of filler hard into the man-made cavity.

Next, a plastic wedge to hold it in place. My mouth cannot possibly open wider without tearing at the edges!

Then when least expected, my dentist asks my opinion about an architectural problem of his . . . it really is very difficult to speak in depth on any subject when somebody else has filled your mouth with about eight fingers and various other items of dental equipment. I grunt but the questions keep on flowing through the cotton mask covering his mouth.

More pushing, more probing, an extra finger, two more plastic dividing strips and another mix of filler, yet, still no pain . . . I can't believe it!

My fear of dentists can be pinpointed to a 'bad experience' during my early teens in Tasmania.

It wasn't until I came to Victoria to play VFL football with Melbourne that I regained some confidence in these 'madmen with drills'. I'm still not super confident about them even though mine's a good bloke.

I had no alternative. I needed a mouth-guard to protect my teeth while playing football. Only a dentist could supply one personally fitted!

Have you ever tried to keep your mouth shut for five minutes while completely full of a sloppy mix of plaster of Paris? The other problem is to try not to swallow any. The taste is terrible and time passes so slowly.

I don't know why I worried about getting the mouth-guard, because with a nose as large as mine — the first item on my face that was going to get into trouble was my nose (five times broken) . . . and I must admit I'm not getting any better looking!

Anyway . . . drilling is almost completed in the dentist's chair. My lip feels fatter than ever and as the time is 11.30 a.m. — will there be any feeling there by 6 p.m.? Because that day I was to read the sports news on Channel 9?

The plastic separating strips are painlessly removed from between my teeth and a file or similar tool is used to shape the filling flush with the original tooth surface.

The water drill has worked, unlike the painful machines of old.

Gee, it must have been bad in the early days of colonisation, when decaying teeth were wrenched from terrified patients with a pair of pliers — sometimes a knee to the throat helped the dentist get more leverage on his patient's jaw!

I believe the first drills were pedal-powered and they provided an awful 'slow grind' and the constant smell of burning teeth.

So much for the past!

The only ordeal remaining for me was a high powered polish!

Still no pain . . . I can't believe it . . . a quick rinse into the miniature water closet, and I'll be okay. Sure, there was some blood but I could handle the blood. You little beauty, It's almost over!

Another dribbling session on to my bib, and I'll be away . . . I sat up and stretched my arms which had been locked tightly around my ribs for the previous hour.

In six months time there will be another check-up, but this time I won't be so frightened!

Thanks, Doc!

Facing the Wardrobe like a Man
'THE MORE WE GET, THE MORE WE WANT'

Isn't it amazing how many problems go away when the 'junk' in your life disappears. Once something is eliminated, its capacity to clutter and mess up your day or your home, or most importantly your life, is gone, I only wish I'd realised that painful truth years ago.

I don't mind owning up to the fact that I grew up in a family that always believed in hanging on to all kinds of junk, just in case it might come in handy for something in the future.

Keeping stuff still seemed reasonable as I grew older. When my drawers, shelves and cupboards were filled, I followed the example of other people and got more drawers. I built more shelves and even elevated my bed so that I could hide and store more 'good junk' underneath it.

There are even people I know who have used the services of an architect to design elaborate storage spaces, in the form of a 'house extension' for the sole purpose of housing excess possessions.

I suppose most people are the same — we set out to attain the pleasures, places and things that we want, when and where we want them. Most of us do just that: Attain, accumulate, collect. Enough is never enough. The more we get; the more we want.

The big crunch comes when we realise what all that comfort, convenience and 'stuff' costs. We have to pay for it, keep track of it, protect it, clean it, store it, insure it and worry about it.

There doesn't appear to be any time left to have some good old fashioned fun and a laugh or two . . .

If we're not careful, not only will our houses, drawers, cupboards and motor cars become so crowded that it's difficult to breathe. Our minds, emotions and personal relationships will buckle at the weight of all of our junk with the result being — dull, boring and stagnant people too preoccupied with possession mania.

Sometimes I sit back in my chair and look at a desk piled with clutter — bills, letters, assignments, newspapers, research, and filing material etc. and think, "What am I doing this for? I should be trying to master a 3-iron on the golf course."

Anyway I decided things must change — I felt exhilarated and keen to get on with the job of dejunking. But where would I begin?

I decided on the wardrobe — there must have been a small fortune invested on the various shaped coathangers that caused the hanging rail to sag badly under the weight.

The fashions ranged through flared trousers, stove-pipes, sloppy joes and wide-lapelled suits. Somehow I'd gathered all these clothes (some were 20 years old) packed them tighter and tighter into the limited space with never any chance of wearing them out. I suppose being fashion conscious is an even greater waste than greed is.

I even had a dinner suit, shirt and bow-tie I purchased at a bargain basement sale the first year I arrived in Melbourne as a skinny adolescent lad in 1967 . . . needless to say, I couldn't get near them today. I've blossomed into a big boy just as my dad suggested I would.

So out they went — trousers, suits, jackets and shirts — even some that I'd worn to the ground on the day I'd taken heaps of wickets or made a few runs — lucky or not, I just had to let go. I almost cried as I stuffed a couple of my well-worn beauties into the green, plastic garbage bag.

My theory used to be that if I wore a certain shirt on a particular day to a sporting event, then I'd be successful. Amazingly, nine times out of ten it seemed to work. Actually instead of telling myself to be a winner in the true mode of all positive thinkers, I used to wear my lucky shirts. But since I wasn't going to be playing Test cricket anymore and they wouldn't fit me anyway, it was bye bye to some treasured Alan Solley shirts.

Next to go were the squadrons of shoes — platform soles, chisel toes, worn-out runners, football boots, buckled cricket boots, thongs — you name them, I probably had at least two of each to discard.

By this time I was into the third plastic bag . . . all destined for one of the St. Vincent de Paul opportunity shops in Melbourne. How does that adage go? 'One man's junk is another man's treasure.'

Wherever they ended up didn't really matter, as long as they didn't lob back in my wardrobe.

I shouldn't forget to mention the ties — literally hundreds of 'em; skinny ones, wide ones, loud ones and plain ones; I was never going to tie the knot in these ghastly accessories, so, like a big bag of small multi-colored off-cuts, out the door they went.

Along with the ties went 23 single socks — without mates or holes. I've got no idea where the other half of each pair disappeared to . . . probably thin air like most missing items in our house.

So there's the challenge, face up to your wardrobe like a man or a woman should, with doors wide open, lights at full bore, and say to yourself, "Why should I keep it?"

You'll probably end up with two piles after leaving all the clothes that you wear regularly and feel good in.

Pile one is the lot that needs to be mended — at least there's some practical reason for not wearing an item. Pile two — out of style, won't fit or you just plain don't want to know about this lot anymore.

Possibly after a second look at the first pile of clobber, you'll end up with a few of these pieces in pile two as well.

When you think about it, junk really is everywhere — open up your wallet and a great wad of mostly useless business cards falls out with numerous other bits of paper.

Open the boot of your car and the odds are it's a beaut space for extra rims, hub caps, jacks, gravel-dented, old, insect-splattered number plates and cardboard boxes.

And inside the car — well that's no better — a filing cabinet for old parking stickers and unpaid fines, antique gas bill receipts, peanut shells, drink cans, crushed fast food containers and tissue boxes, sweet wrappers, directions to last month's party, single lensed sunglasses, dried out first-aid kits and a bottle opener.

Yes it would be fair to say that some of the finest clutter collections in the world are hoarded in the confines of our cars.

And how embarrassing it is to have so much clutter, clobber, trash or whatever that you don't even remember where it all is. Having extra vacuum cleaner bags, fuses, candles, tape measures or scales, are of no use when you can't find them!

When I don't know where something is, I'll dig like a hungry dog for a bone trying to unearth it and tear up every storage space in the whole house to get it.

My study used to be a real mess . . . in fact it was quite intimidating to just walk into the room. Piles of magazines, newspapers, folders, letters and boxes of stationery enclosed the work space, desperate for a home, or even just to be acknowledged. Everyone keeps old magazines and newspapers but what about all those less obvious stray bits of paper?

Have you ever noticed how people must keep expired life insurance policies? Just in case re-incarnation might occur in reverse. We paid too much for it. It looks so legal. We'd better keep it!

The other old faithful piece of paper that's never thrown out is the raffle ticket. The fact that we keep it, though it was drawn in 1973, I suppose indicates that human hope never dies (as long as we keep junk around to remind us).

How much unopened junk mail, how many outdated catalogues and newsletters, obsolete timetables, old lists, worn out slogan stickers, wrinkled posters and old Christmas cards and calendars, half-filled out questionnaires, old competition entry forms and magazine subscription offers, outdated reports, box tops, expired coupons and unidentifiable envelopes of 'stuff' do you have stashed away somewhere? In my case they're all based under and on top of a bench in my study.

Yes I've even got unused 1981/82/83/84/85 diaries that might come in handy — when? Also there's ancient address books . . . I know I'll never use them.

Now, let me see, where will I start?

Carry On Doctor

'TOO MUCH SITTING DOWN AND TALKING. NOT ENOUGH EXERCISE AND DOING'

It's often been said that a person's body is merely a vehicle to travel from birth to death in!

It's our own choice whether or not we choose to make that journey, in an aerodynamically designed machine, similar to a Formula One racing car, or maybe we're just happy to get along on a daily basis in a beat-up old jalopy that doesn't take too much looking after!

And just like all motor cars, no matter how old or how new, our bodies also need constant attention and sometimes a major overhaul.

Well, I had a look at my calendar, and realised it had been about three years since I had my last full-scale doctor's check-up. And judging by the speedometer that continually whirrs inside my head, I could sense my visit to the Shepherd Foundation Health Testing Clinic, in colourful Fitzroy St., St. Kilda, was long overdue.

For example, during the 1985-86 summer, Channel 9 cricket commentators clocked up almost 50,000 km each in air-travel between capital city match venues and towards the end of the season, we all needed another aeroplane ride like a hole in the head!

A phone call confirmed the appointment. The whole exercise takes about two hours. But the strict discipline and dieting procedures expected prior to arrival at the centre, are similar to what super coach Tom Hafey would expect of his high flying Sydney Swans, the night before a big match! Difficult for a man like myself in the twilight of his sporting career.

"Please avoid any excessive alcohol consumption." That was just the beginning!

It is necessary that you fast for eight-16 hours before eating a 'special meal' that must be commenced exactly one hour, 45 minutes prior to your appointment time.

As my appointment was scheduled for 10 a.m., I was told to commence my last normal meal at 7.00 p.m. on the previous night, and then to have no further food or drink until 8.30 a.m. the next morning. I can tell you it was a very dry old night — just thinking about what I couldn't have, made me even thirstier! I felt like a Toohey's or two.

148

Then the last line of the instructions: 'You may satisfy your thirst with water before eating the special meal.' Generous mob aren't they?

In fact I needed a couple of extra glasses of water, to allow myself to swallow the special meal of two slices of dry toast plus a banana and a glass of lemonade. Very exotic stuff and bland too!

Now after drinking all that water and lemonade I almost overlooked another requirement — a painful one too! "Do not pass urine for at least two hours before your appointment.

That's easier said than done, especially with a bladder full of water. In fact, there are very few sensations in the world that will go even close to passing water when you're really under pressure.

All for a good cause and in the end I arrived there fairly relaxed and on time.

The aim of the health testing is directed towards a wide range of medical conditions. Scientific analysis of the test results then helps your doctor evaluate your health and develop a health correction plan if necessary.

I'm not a huge rap for seeing blood at the best of times, so with the blood sample programmed first up, it was just a matter of "Hello, Sister?" Then, tightly clenching my teeth to give me strength. I hate pain, especially from needes so thick in diameter! There was no escape. A sharp turn of my head away from the white-clad woman, quickly labelled me a coward.

"Just a small prick and it'll be all over!" She said with a knowing smile — I'm certain she's hurt many a man before me by puncturing his veins and his ego!

Next was the urine sample. I waited for so long I had almost forgotten how. But not just an ordinary urine sample — no, this one had to be 'mid-stream'. A cute little term isn't it?

"Start. Stop. Collect. And start again" . . . talk about a circus, after a two hour wait.

Then the idea was to discreetly plant my warm little amber-coloured container on the appropriate tray with all the other successful attempts at 'mid-streaming' — embarrassing to say the least! Gee it's moments like this that make me realise how lucky I am to have large concealing hands.

On the other hand it also makes one wonder how some of the world's best athletes get on after competing in a big international event and then being asked to give a compulsory urine sample. I'm told some have stood and addressed the plastic containers for up to three hours before 'winning' the struggle against their body to come forward with a trickle.

Next it was time to clear the wax from my ears with the 'audiometry' or hearing test. Too bad if you don't like being locked up. Into the old-fashioned fridge-like booth I went. Through the glass window I could see my attractive medical technician attending the appropriate gauges necessary to test each patient at six different frequencies of the acoustic spectrum. I'm certain she tried to trick me a couple of times too! But what the nurse didn't realise is that I used to be able to hear a batsman get the

150

faintest of edges — off my own bowling of course — and even when the wind was blowing a gale down the wicket so that the umpire couldn't pick it up! I've lost count of the number of times I've been unlucky, and seen the offending batsman given not out.

Judging by my career batting averages and several indifferent attempts to score a cluster of runs, it would be fair to say I couldn't bat, and probably had problems with my eyes.

Well, I just couldn't wait to get the results of my eyesight tests back. I might have scored full marks there. If so, maybe I ought to be an umpire rather than a commentator. On second thoughts, with the slow motion replays it could be a bad move.

Even a few pounds heavier than my playing weight, I was ready for the 'physical'. Time to get my gear off! But into what was I going to step?

As it turned out, a very flimsy blue paper robe. It was hardly a 46 long — my size! In fact, the length finished a long way above the knees.

I must have looked outrageous! Heaven help me if someone recognises me. And that's exactly what did happen. Here I was having a chat with a fit looking 50-year-old who had just completed some time on the treadmill and another big guy who looked like a moving picture show he had that many tattoos on his body. All of us were conscious of how silly we looked — all three bodies were nothing short of polar bear white.

My height measurement showed up the fact that I had shrunk almost half an inch since I played football, or maybe as an architecture student my hair was much longer?

Weight needs to be lost! Enough said about that. Too much sitting down and talking. Not enough exercise and doing!

These two basic items led me into a breathing exercise — a respiratory test to measure the capacity of my lungs. After one practice run it was fair dinkum stuff. Whilst blocking my nose with my left hand, I had to blow as hard as I could into what looked like an empty toilet roll holder connected to a flexible plastic hose. By the time I'd run out of breath my percentage of lung capacity steadied at 94%. So it's obvious I've lost some wind from the good old days of shouting: "Owzat ump?" Although there are a few people who would argue I'm all wind!

Now for the big one — vital sign tests! Blood pressure was taken and recorded both lying down and standing up!

Television is the sort of industry where blood pressure and tempers are always high on the scale — I'll be interested in the result.

Then while lying down I was prepared for an ECG or what is commonly known as a standard electro-cardiogram. The nurse had me wired for sound, so to speak, and that meant fixing special rubber suction cups onto my ankles, wrists and chest. These were then connected to the machine recording the electrical characteristics of my heart's performance on a graph paper printout.

The sight of tangled wires and suction cups dissecting my motionless

151

body brought some humour from the nurse: "Now you know what it's like making love to an octopus," she said.

I couldn't help but smile and replied: "I bet you're into bondage in your spare time?" There was a deathly silence from the woman in white but her assistant giggled and offered her two bob's worth with, "I dare you to answer that?"

It was all good fun and made the two hours fly and it took my mind off the man next in line, a shivering Chinese patient, who had trouble understanding anything the girls said. I tried not to offend him by laughing, but in the end I couldn't help myself. Some of the situations were straight out of 'Carry on Doctor.'

The sensation of cold glass against my rib cage for the standard chest X-ray brought a different look to my face . . . it was difficult to stand perfectly still because, like my Chinese friend, I was shivering as well, even my teeth were chattering. Who knows, I could be out of focus when the X-rays come back, but one thing is for sure, the pictures will be in black and white!

To finish off the tests we had to answer a wide range of computerised questions about past health conditions and current symptoms in the privacy of a booth and the comfort of a 'cuppa tea and bickies'. They went down very well at the time because it had been about 17 hours — apart from the toast and banana 'special' — between meals.

I'd like to think my body is a Ferrari but I know it's not! But as I get older I do know it's the only one I've got and the only one I'm going to get!

So from here on in I'm going to make sure it gets the best possible treatment.

Why don't you do the same for yours!

The Risk of Smarties

'HE BELIEVED THE YARN ABOUT THE SPECIAL FRENCH BOOSTERS'

All the rewards in sport go to the winners, so it's not difficult to comprehend why the average sports person seeks the quickest and best way to be number one.

As long as I can remember, competitors have been looking for something to give them a winning edge. Now many sportsmen have turned to drugs as a short term answer to improving performance.

Although in my day one of the most common motivating factors behind any quiet request for a 'lift' in the medical room before a game, was usually to conceal the previous night's resulting hangover!

A wonderful illustration of this familiar ritual happened more than a decade ago in Adelaide when VFL premiership team Richmond was competing in a series to decide the outright Australian champion team.

To cut accommodation costs, three matches were played in a week with very little rest for players. This lack of recovery time particularly worried Brian Roberts, the giant Richmond ruckman known as 'The Whale'! He was not looking forward to spending another four quarters chasing the ball from goal post to goal post, with only one day's rest and a fairly big night behind him!

An hour before play he sidled up to the club's head-trainer and asked if he had anything to help him get through the day. Well, The Whale was lucky!

He was told it was too early for a pill and to come back in 30 minutes. In the meantime a messenger was sent to pick up a box of Smarties. The cunning head-trainer selected two orange Smarties and waited! The mentally and physically fatigued player soon whispered the question, "Okay now?" into the receptive ear.

Brian's head was banging from a truck load the night before, and he was prepared to do anything to get through the match. He believed the yarn, about the special 'French Boosters' being very bitter to taste if not swallowed immediately. Yep, The Whale downed the two pills and prepared to 'take-off'.

It has often been stated that winning or losing is a state of mind! The effect on the man who had represented three states at football was astonishing. The big fella rucked all day and kicked some amazing goals to be almost best player afield.

Brian Roberts, now a successful hotel proprietor in Melbourne, still enjoys an ale. And his clientele love to talk him through the day he got high on Smarties.

Unfortunately the drug problem in sport has become deadly serious. The death of two young American sports stars in 1986 from cocaine abuse focused attention on the need for mandatory drug testing.

Today U.S. sporting authorities must contend with an endless stream of amateur psychologists, do-gooders and parochial club lawyers, who use the constitution of civil rights arguments to try to avoid the introduction of widespread mandatory drug tests.

Initially used to discern illicit means of attaining a competitive edge, the tests are now being adapted to detect the residue of 'social drugs' capable of adversely affecting field performances and destroying lives.

Australian sportsmen and women may not use cocaine quite as extensively as their U.S. counterparts, but the Co-ordinator of Drugs in Sport Campaign for the Australian Sports Commission, Steve Haynes, says that it is largely a question of money.

"American professional sportsmen are paid much more. A common attitude is: 'if you have got a quid to spare put it into cocaine'. Australian sportsmen are not earning so much money, but as wages rise, the chances for people using drugs will also rise."

The history of sport is full of stories detailing effects of additive performance. Morphine has helped athletes put up with pain. Testosterone has worked on muscles and tissues for greater strength and improved recuperation. Amphetamines have stimulated the body/mind performance. Adrenalin has activated, and caffeine has worked to stimulate the central nervous system.

Yet all of these drug additives are specifically banned in sport for good reason.

Some drugs are not detectable, like vitolin, which was used by the U.S. swimmers in the early '70s and is a legitimate drug prescribed for hyperactive children.

Nevertheless the cold hard facts are that all drugs have more or less harmful effects, depending on the dosage. This explains why some people have indulged with impunity, yet others have suffered greatly.

Anabolic steroids, for instance, when taken under medical supervision, have helped many elderly people recover from broken limbs. However, such dosages are small — 5-10 mg a day — and discontinued immediately the repair operations are under way.

A world champion discus thrower in the '70s admitted taking 900 mg a day for periods of up to eight months. He is now sterile: his skin is covered in rashes and there is suspicion that he has liver cancer.

Steroids are synthetic male hormones which act on our growth gland, the pituitary, to regulate the size of cells in the muscles, and other tissues. And they work! Research has confirmed that they increase body mass and muscular development. They increase red cell production in blood and enable a quicker recovery from injury.

Evidence of the bad effects of steroids on the world's sportsmen and women is more serious than ever. A 'foreign report' named 59 Soviet athletes who have perished since 1952 from traumas directly associated with anabolic steroids abuse. The list includes 18 gold medallists, the most famous of whom was Alexander Belov, hero of the 1972 basketball gold medal team, who died in 1978, aged 27.

Steroids have also been used to retard puberty in female gymnasts.

The dilemma for sports people who select the steroid path is whether to risk health for the glory of victory or choose anonymity.

A more recent 'second cousin' to steroids is the human growth hormone, HgH. Its supply has been limited until recently when synthetic varieties have been developed. It also promises strength increase but brings with it serious problems such as diabetes, hepatitis and in some cases giantism.

The practice, too, of blood doping has received prominence.

Typically the distance runner withdraws a litre of blood several months before the planned performance peak. This blood is frozen and stored to be re-injected days before the race. As the body naturally restores the lost litre in the interim, the re-injected blood boosts the athlete's circulatory fluid, increasing the number of red cells, thus helping store more oxygen.

This procedure is also banned, as overload in the 'pump system' can cause related problems.

Some sports persons have assumed that recreational drugs like marijuana and hashish are safe.

This is a dangerous assumption as these drugs increase heart rate and blood pressure, impair motor co-ordination and sensory functions, interfere with short-term memory and increase anxiety, confusion and even produce psychosis.

The decision whether or not to take drugs is a personal one and unfortunately not always well informed.

For mine, the best advice a young sportsman or woman can receive is education on the adverse effects that go hand in hand with usage.

So you can see, drugs in sport are a very serious problem, something we can all do without. The answer is simple: don't use them!

Hooked on the Grand Final
'EVERYONE ON THE GROUND IS HIGH AS A KITE'

There is not a Saturday during the average Australian's sports calendar to compare with the VFL Grand Final Day.

The first game of VFL football I attended just happened to be the 1966 grand final played between Collingwood and St. Kilda.

I couldn't have wished for a more enthralling game of football — the result went right down to the wire. With only seconds remaining, St. Kilda's forward Barry Breen scored a solitary point, as the siren sounded, to win the action-packed game for the Saints!

As for myself, I was jubilant — even though, a few weeks earlier I had partly realised a childhood ambition and signed a contract to play with the prestigious Melbourne Football Club, I was still cheering for the Saints! This was mainly due to the St. Kilda team having several Tasmanians playing in their line-up. So why not support my hometown boys . . . names like Baldock and Stewart!

From that Saturday afternoon I became hooked on VFL football — and like thousands of teenage footballers right across the country, I became even more determined to play senior football.

Looking back on my career as a sportsman, one of my few disappointments was not to have run on to the sacred MCG turf late in September for the Melbourne team to play in a VFL grand final.

Just for the record, Melbourne haven't played in a Grand Final since their win over Collingwood in 1964.

Nevertheless it has been my almost habitual pleasure to witness live as a spectator, almost all of the VFL premierships contested in the last 19 years.

Just to be in the crowd is a moving experience in more ways than one — especially if you've had too many beers, and are located in the 'standing room only' area. When you've got to breathe in harmony with the guys either side of you as well as in the front and back, it doesn't matter how desperately nature calls, the honest truth is, the toilets really are too far away!

And some of the stories about standing in the outer on half-a-dozen empty beer cans to get a better view, are obviously true! Good luck if you've got standing room only tickets — the 'go' is not to drink too much at all! Isn't it?

If you're lucky and have a reserved seat, then by all means take your vacuum flask of soup and a few sandwiches for half time and life will be a ball. Mind you, it's not as good as being one of the lucky ones in the selected few 'super boxes'.

I've never been in one, but they tell me it's 'champagne and chicken' or whatever turns you on. Even slow motion replays on the closed circuit television — but that's not really what a day at the footy should be all about! Well, certainly not in my family.

No matter what the sporting event, the magic of being there on the day can't be matched by the technological advances in television. I think it's best described as 'atmosphere'! The air of anticipation in the minutes before the players run on to the ground is incredible . . . the buzz in the air is thick enough to eat.

Beneath the grandstands the players go through their last minute rituals. Even the boot studders and masseurs are nervous . . . they can do no more for the 20 selected players dressed in their club colors.

At last the vigorous warm up exercises are complete — almost 365 days preparation lies behind them as they tuck in their jumpers for the battle. Arms and legs of 20 beautifully trained athletes glisten below the globes hanging alone in the property stewards' room — this is the venue for the coach's pre-match address. Just a few short metres away in the adjacent dressing rooms, the opposition camp will be going through a similar ordeal.

The rooms are cleared of any persons other than players or club officials at the coach's loud, abrasive demand!

The key man would have been pacing the locker room floor for almost an hour prior to this moment, in an effort to assemble in his head the most important verbal barrage, or pre-game talk, to his players for the entire season.

"Look at me, every one of you . . ." The talk would last approximately five minutes, building in volume and intensity until everyone in earshot becomes glassy-eyed, tense and ready to run through a brick wall to bring success. "Give me blood, I want blood today!"

This is the point where the players can no longer blame the coach — he got them into the final — only they can win it.

Every player has to decide in the next 100 minutes whether or not he's going to be a spectator or a player in one of the toughest physical contact sports played anywhere in the world — Australian football.

The fanfare now begins, as players are pushed forward by pure adrenalin and a fiercely pumping heart. They run down the race on to the well manicured grass surface and through the huge, colourful, cheer squad banners — these take many days to make and yet are broken in just a couple of seconds!

Before the start, a massive roar echoes around the stadium . . . immediately hundreds of gas filled balloons begin their assault on the stratosphere, like 'hundreds and thousands' covering the sky above the stadium.

The umpire holds the egg-shaped football above his head and with a sharp burst of air into his whistle, the game is finally under way.

For the first 15 minutes of the first quarter everyone on the ground is as high as a kite, floating on cloud nine and operating on the pure hype provided by the occasion and the crowd noise. For everyone it will be an experience never to forget!

After the initial shock, the game will settle down a bit as the players get what is known as their 'second wind'.

The fitter a player is, the sooner his second wind arrives and that terrible heart-burn disappears.

Players run at the ball and each other with total disregard for body and limb . . . a win on this day makes all the blood, sweat and tears expended in the 22 home and away games plus other finals, worth it.

Unfortunately only one team can win. To run second on this day would certainly leave a nasty scar for the rest of your life. Ask Collingwood — their players carry more scars than any other VFL team.

To sit in the shadow of more than 100,000 people whilst watching your opponents accept their victory medals, would have to leave a bad taste in your mouth.

But to see the losing coach shake hands with his opposite number is truly a heart-warming sight, especially in the world of bad sportsmanship we share today.

The ultimate sensation for the winning team and the spectators is to watch the ecstatic victory lap by the winning team as each player takes a turn at showing the large, shiny Premiership Cup to every sector of the crowd amidst hugs and self congratulations. The exhilaration really shows.

Even sitting far away in the crowded grandstand, the hair on the back of my neck stands up at this stage.

Then, the lump in my throat gets larger, and the possiblity of my eyes welling up becomes real. I can relate the glory of victory these guys are now sharing to some great sporting memories of my own!

A Lot of Chook Raffles

'IT'S NOT HARD TO SAY NO TO A SMOKE OR DRINK . . .'

The average Australian loves his or her sport no matter what their age. But as we rapidly move towards the year 2000, what is the future of sport? Or should I say, sport as we used to know it!

It's all very well to turn back the clock to the great old days when kids used to play cricket in the street using an old rubbish tin for wickets and a piece of fence paling for a bat, or when they kicked a battered old football made up of unloved stockings. Those days are now gone!

I was lucky enough to pursue a career in two professional sports — cricket and football. Now I look back on the past 20 years, from a schoolboy sportsman, VFL footballer, international cricketer and today a sporting commentator with Channel Nine.

There has been a far reaching change in almost every sport I care to mention due to the power of the mighty dollar and sponsorship.

Today the heavyweight sport sponsors are the alcohol and tobacco industries. Between them they account for almost half the cash sponsorship of Australian sport. And most importantly they reinforce that link with huge advertising budgets.

The tobacco industry is the largest sponsor accounting for about 25 per cent. And despite the common cry from the anti-smoking lobby, the industry was a heavily committed sponsor well before cigarette advertising was banned on both television and radio in 1976.

I wonder how many people know that Rothmans helped to stage the 1956 Melbourne Olympic Games? And it should be noted that during the Games there wasn't an advertising sign saying 'Smoke Rothmans' anywhere in sight!

I'm not a smoker. Never have been! Well, to be truthful, when I was eight years old, I got caught nicking a few packets out of my mum's shop. I am very pleased to say, after my subsequent thrashing on the bare buttocks, I haven't touched one since. Except for maybe the odd cigar after the birth of my three sons and occasionally after a special Test match win.

The most recent example of multi-million dollar sponsorship has been the marriage between Australia's greatest horse racing event, the Melbourne Cup, and the blue and white Foster's beer can. The name change to 'The Foster's Melbourne Cup' is not entirely unrelated to the fact that a substantial proportion of the stake money which rocketed from $500,000 to the magical $1 million, was supplied by the makers of the famous amber fluid.

I believe that the sponsorship of the prestigious Melbourne Cup was inevitable. It was a large but a very predictable step in a continuing process which has seen sport of many varieties turn to business houses for much needed support during the last decade.

The Foster's Melbourne Cup merger is symbolically at least, the ultimate Australian sports sponsorship. A coming together of two Melbourne institutions with a view to mutual benefits. And that's exactly what happened.

Basically I believe very strongly in sports sponsorship. I'm sure the following figures will explain just how much our sport relies on the dollars and cents injected by the corporate sector.

To the end of June 1985, for example, the Federal Government spent a total of $55 million on our sport. But by comparison, figures available from the Confederation of Australian Sport suggest that the commercial sector spent $57 million in direct cash sponsorship alone, and that doesn't count horse-racing.

Now, not only does the racing industry account for several million dollars more in direct sponsorship, but sponsors individually spend a further $260 million in advertising which clearly reinforces the sports image.

After all, why shouldn't the corporate sector want to be associated with a nice, clean healthy, sports image? That's really what sponsorship is all about: image making. Identifying a product with something exciting, like sport.

The sponsors generally like to retain a special interest in sports which use their products (like car racing) but many others adopt a particular sport to help sell a vast range of products, and I suppose to project an image of being successful, public spirited, even patriotic.

This is relevant when we look at VFL football. In 1984, car maker Nissan locked up a deal spending big money on VFL football. It was a good move by Nissan to identify with a fair dinkum Aussie sport like Australian football.

But at the end of the line, it would be fair to say that the business houses injecting money into sport must get a decent run for their support. It must be both give and take, something for everyone.

In 1985 one of the most controversial sponsorship deals was the takeover of the Sydney Swans by Dr Geoffrey Edelstein.

Being an old footballer in the days of the running dropkick and Ron Barassi, I keep a bit of an eye on the scene, and I must admit I don't like what I see happening in the VFL. In fact I believe if VFL football is to survive, the Sydney Swans must fail, or more to the point, go bankrupt. I reckon the Sydney Swans exercise had indirectly inflated player-payments to around 50 per cent more than is realistic for their worth.

There are a lot of fringe footballers around now employing accountants, agents, lawyers or 'Mr Ten Percenters' who have advised their players to mention, rather bluntly, that they've been talking to other clubs. Usually with the desired effect — more dollars in next year's contract. That is making a lot of clubs edgy and poorer.

And that's why there is so much talk of clubs wanting to merge. The simple truth is that a city the size of Melbourne can't support 12 clubs who have all got to find somewhere between $4-6 million just to stay alive. That's a lot of chook raffles, eh?

Soon the crunch will come with most clubs saying: 'Look, that's it, we can honestly only afford $X for your services'. I believe that's already happening at a few clubs but if the wealthy clubs successfully stay in the buying market, then it will make a solution very difficult for the VFL.

Sponsorship is a subject that could be discussed forever and it probably will be. But I hope those people who are lobbying against the tobacco companies and breweries realise the significance of the corporate dollar to sport sponsorship and our young people. Sport involves something like 20,000 clubs, six million people, and all these people are better for their involvement.

People will still smoke and drink, whether the tobacco industry or breweries sponsor sport or not. My reasoning is that sponsorship in sport will make more people healthy by that money being used effectively in sport.

It's not hard to say no to a smoke or a drink if you care to, but it will be very difficult to find $30 million in a hurry. And we won't get it from our politicians, will we?